Great Food for Happy Kids

RENDEZVOUS PRESS

Toronto, Canada

Great Food
for Happy Kids

by
Jesse Frayne

illustrated by
Gina Calleja

with a foreword by
Marni Jackson

RendezVous Press
Toronto Ontario Canada
www.rendezvouspress.com
distributed by Pearson PTR Canada

Printed and bound in Canada

06 05 04 03 02 01   5 4 3 2 1

National Library of Canada Cataloguing in Publication Data

Frayne, Jesse, date-
  Great food for happy kids

ISBN 0-929141-75-X

1. Cookery. 2. Children—Nutrition. I. Calleja, Gina II. Title

TX652.F2 2001   641.5'622   C2001-930217-7

Acknowledgments

I am enormously grateful to Joanna Watts: she decided we needed this book, and over time we evolved together its format. She has been my dear friend for twenty years. A few of the recipes are Joanna's, but all of the feeling is thanks to her. She has given me her support through thin and thin, she throws about the best party that can be thrown, and I hope that we will know each other all our lives.

I must thank Marni Jackson for her lovely foreword. She is a steady ally, an uncommonly generous woman and a dervish on the violin. My darling mom, June Callwood, has seen me through this and many other manuscripts. Her advice is always the right advice and is always given kindly. My husband Mark Manchester, who puzzles me with his loyalty, is the recipient of the Hall of Fame Medal for Patience.

A craft is learned. Our influences become part of our learning on a level that is sometimes almost subconscious. Though I have attempted to give credit to my many teachers, if I have failed in this aim, I would be grateful to be put straight and given the chance to make amends in the next reprint.

FOREWORD

by Marni Jackson

I was blessed with a son who eats. Last one asleep on the maternity floor, the day he was born...slurp, slurp, slurp. Then home and breastfeeding around the clock, until I felt like I was merely the vertical appendage, the human trolley, that trundled The Breasts in and out of his room. Solids? No problem: shreddies on the highchair tray, apple slices, the odd slice of prosciutto. Well, the prosciutto was an accident, but as it turned out, he loved it.

So I never had to do the here-comes-the plane-into-the-hangar thing. But I did have to deal with his asthma, and his allergies. As a result, I was forever tinkering with his diet, eliminating this or that...and yearning for a sensible, sensual, kid-centric cookbook like this one. The trick here is that the author is not just knowledgeable on the food front, but wise in the ways of kids.

◆   ◆   ◆

At four, my son became the eager food adventurer, relishing Indian daal, plain yogurt, and mysterious creatures in black bean sauce. Not that I was cooking all these things. At the time, I was working in an office job and not above coming home to "cook" Kraft dinner, served (to assuage my conscience) with "trees" (broccoli, with a shake of parmesan) and a "salad" (sliced tomatoes). To this day he has a soft spot for the violent orange emollient of a nice bowl of Kraft dinner.

It doesn't get more elementary than that, and on the nights when you don't care to assay California handrolls, a parent wants, um, permission to open cans, or to rip open boxes. (The author draws the line at boxes in this book, but she does let mothers off the hook in other delicious ways.)

Now my son is seventeen, and an old hand vegetarian. I am too, sort of, but his father likes to be thrown the odd bit of meat. So the dinner conundrum remains. We eat lots of fish, barbecued, even if it means the barbecuer has to step through snowdrifts to get to the grill. And yes, I can do couscous with chickpeas for Tofu Boy and then throw in curried chicken for us…but what about the challenge of packing five non-boring vegetarian school lunches a week? This is where my friend, neighbour and food inspiration Jesse Frayne comes in.

Right now I am thinking about the sandwiches Jesse packed for us when we set off on a weekend canoe trip recently—my son, her twin teenage daughters, their aunt and me.

We'd been driving for four hours when the picnic was deployed. My sandwich was grilled eggplant, marinated red pepper and provolone cheese, between chewy slices of fresh sourdough bread. There was red pepper draped on the steering wheel. And avocado and tomato salad, bathed in the dreamiest vinaigrette, came with it. I discovered that a salad is remarkably easy to eat with your fingers, while driving down a bumpy dirt road—if it tastes good enough, which it did. "This is the best sandwich I've ever eaten," my son flatly declared.

Other Jesse meals I recall fondly: a simple flank steak basted in something fine and cooked in the oven, that made me, in my meat days, a flank steak fan thereafter (at least until we hit the Meat Wall); a winter fondue around her dining room table; a New Year's Eve when she arrived with a platter of the freshest of Vietnamese spring rolls, full of greens with bite—radish sprouts? and a fiery dipping sauce in the middle. We've had some ripsnorting neighbourhood parties, and Jesse's cooking has been what sustains us.

Jesse has lived around the corner from our family since my son was small. She has four children from the ages twelve to nineteen, each one with the cool, discerning palate of a Tuscany wine-taster, even Jack, an expert on Cheez-Doodles, who wouldn't touch a sprout with a ten-foot pole. The sentence I most like to hear from Jesse, if I am calling about some gathering, is "What can I bring?" I know that it will be the best, the most original, and zingiest thing on the table. It will not look like she spent hours making spun-sugar gazebos for it. It will look like fresh, real food, it will taste bright, surprising and somehow thoughtful, and above all, the children in the room will eat it.

I have memories of Jesse in three different kitchens. When I first met her, she was the new mother of twin baby girls and working out of her house as a caterer for film crews. Try that combo sometime—making coleslaw for ninety-five, with twin toddlers underfoot. Next, Jesse lived in a house around the corner, with a kitchen the size of a Toyota dashboard. Great dishes came out of that kitchen, a reminder that nobody needs copper pots and overhead racks to cook well. Now she lives but a block further, in a house with a larger, farmhouse sort of kitchen, big enough for the aquariums, fifties' lamps and children's artwork that are essential to her kitchens. She served us homemade pizzas and baked fennel in that kitchen a few weeks back.

My son now politely declines most of our invitations to join us at some adult dinner party, but when it involves Jesse's cooking, he is there. Her daughters are growing up into easy, expert cooks too. The only family hold-out is the youngest, Jack. Jack is a hot dog man and proud of it. Oh, how sharper than a serpent's tooth are the eating habits of our young. Books like this one offer inspiration, solace and solutions.

BEGINNINGS

What do kids want? This is the important question. You mull it over at three a.m., walking the hall with your sobbing infant. You drag it out when you get the wrong Barbie for her birthday. You shake your head when you're in there buying the lacy brassiere, the right goalie pads. Over time, a few conclusions arise.

Mainly, kids want a warm place to snuggle up to.

They want acceptance and information. They want respect and space. Instruction, recreation, diversion and counsel are in there somewhere, but these are not things that children long for. They long for autonomy from the very first year, with your steady background hum, your discreet shelter along the way. They want to push the envelope, they want you to set the boundaries.

Small kids want to look at pictures of themselves when they were smaller. They want to check with you occasionally that they are getting bigger. They want to find ways in which you, parent and child, are the same, and later, ways in which you are different. Your life together starts as close as you can be, the most intimate bond, and over time you are expected to back off. This is hard, but you get a lot of help from nature.

Kids want you to help them physically when their small bodies are uncooperative, but they want you to get your hands off when they are able to try out things for themselves. Today they can't get the bike to go at all unless you're holding the seat, tomorrow they'd rather die than have you touch the darn thing. Today the shoelaces, tomorrow the subway.

And through their lives, from infancy to high school, from moving out to moving back in, Thanksgiving to Labour Day, they want to eat.

◆   ◆   ◆

In the fifties, there were six ways to have food. There were no other lettuces besides iceberg. Pot roast was party fare, and vegetables meant sliced carrots, tinned peas and boiled potatoes. In those cloistered days, milk, butter and eggs were delivered to the door. The breadman brought sugar donuts, the doctor made housecalls with his black satchel. Mothers stayed home. We did as we were told.

Authority was very big. Our parents didn't question professionals, we didn't question our parents. Women gave birth unconscious. Dr. Spock had us all weaned to formula right away and toilet trained at six months. We gave street directions politely to strangers. We ate all our dinners. We were strapped tight against polio, tuberculosis and world war, and our parents struggled to pay their twenty-five year mortgages.

Whereas now, there are plump and velvety little lettuces flown daily, from the other side of the world, to the corner store. We have the mobility, discretion and income to choose how the international influences, environmental standards and sensual appeal will tempt our families tonight.

But the puzzling thing is, Bobby wants hot dogs, and in the nineties it's his right to eat what he wants.

Authority is out the window, individual expression is very big.

Mom and Dad are having a nice goat korma with homemade puri, Sis prefers Stouffers. Uncle John's on a no-fat, no cholesterol diet, Auntie May is building protein, Sabrina is allergic to sugar and milk and wheat, Danny had cola, chips and gravy for his high school lunch, Grampa's on a book tour eating pasta in restaurants, and Granny's at an opening at the Met, with cocktails and lovely stuffed pastry puffs.

Families don't always eat together any more, but they crave it just the same. In the dizzying shimmer of choice and chase and overload, the core of family life is still comfort. Kids thrive in it, parents stretch their socked feet and sigh deeply over it, friends drop over and stay late, basking in it. Food is the stimulus for discussion, exchange, relief and satisfaction.

When you get a chance, you make something delicious, you don't kill yourself doing it, and the family sits together and shares life for a while. The baby in the highchair sprinkles beansprouts in her hair and practices consonants, the suspicious four-year-old is relieved, the eight-year-old with the food phobia gets enough to grow, the teenager straightens us out on a few relevant matters while eating everything in sight, the boomer enjoys the taste, the mother-in-law is a good sport. This is my favourite meal.

◆   ◆   ◆

With this book, we wanted to cover everything about food for kids. Breastfeeding your newborn is a wonderful and expedient system of perfect nourishment that sometimes doesn't work out, and you opt for another system. And your babies grow! They pat their hands on their highchair trays and await pablum.

Divide up the age groups for eating and you might get, as we did, the experimental set, age 2 to 6; and then the gregarious ones, 8 to 12, and the older ones who want to prepare things alone. So the early recipes in this book are low-key and they set up the later ones.

In every chapter there's a nod to kids who have modern allergies, the environmental kinds that are afflicting urban children. Careful diagnosis and dietary changes are helping many kids, and while this is far better than the endless doses of antibiotic, it's tough to find food they can enjoy. Herein you will find some ideas on dietary substitutions.

Many people spend their first twenty or thirty years setting up their lives just like they want their lives to be, and then they give birth to some little squirt who changes everything. We trade over every personal goal, every expectation. We learn what vulnerability is. We can't believe we can hurt so much, or love so much. Isn't that nature's way? Keeps things interesting.

Our kids are so precious to us, so confounding and absorbing. We want to show them support, we want the world to get better. We're starting small.

It's the start of someone big. Today the infant, tomorrow the world. Let there be pink balloons and lots of survivors. Let there be food on the table that they can enjoy. Let there be harbour at home.

GREAT FOOD
FOR HAPPY KIDS

CHAPTER ONE

Fingerfoods

There are not that many recipes for breastmilk, and formula is also limited in culinary scope. So we begin our cookbook with fingerfoods, which you coincidentally prepare as you putter in the kitchen, your little one studying you expectantly from her highchair. Small babies start with stuff that has no lumps. You can buy puréed babyfood in any grocery store. And, if you have time, or if you want to supplement your child's diet with fresh food, you can make your own.

Organic vegetables of any kind, steamed gently, buzzed in the blender, served. It takes minutes. Add a blob of tofu, there's the protein. It's not much trouble, and it feels great.

Homemade applesauce, or fresh squeezed oranges, or strawberries and bananas buzzed together on the spot. It's easy. And stuff saved as autumn comes on, individual servings frozen in icecube trays, or three servings frozen together in those little jars. Swiss chard from your garden, carrots, beans, squash, picked at its seasonal peak. Heavenly.

I don't mind buying jars of meat from the grocery. I could never get my meat ground up fine enough at home, and the kids wouldn't eat it. This would be your bottom line: *that the kids eat.* Maybe you know a way to do meat that works for you. Maybe you'll tell ME. At the time, I closed my eyes to the commercial nature of the product. Convenience prevailed. I'm a normal person.

When babies begin to get teeth, they gnaw on things to relieve their tingling gums. Isn't Nature clever? Babies can feed themselves stuff even at seven or eight months of age. Foods that dissolve are best at first, of course, like teething biscuits and bread crusts, but the precedent gets set up in their little minds and as time goes by and the teeth erupt, they chew on more complicated, binary code, net-surfing things. By eleven or twelve months of age, babies can manage some pretty fantastic nutrition. (*recipes to follow)

yogourt, egg custard* and rice pudding*
small chunks of soft cheese
large-curd cottage cheese
grilled cheese on whole wheat toast squares
hummos* on whole wheat toast or pita
brown rice fried with a scrambled egg*, and a drop of
   Kikkoman
pancakes*, crepes* or blintzes*, cut up, with syrup or
   applesauce*
Cheerios, shreddies, dry or with milk
whole sautéed chicken livers* (organic!)
crumbled cooked burger (chicken or whoever), (eek, even
   McDonald's)

17

small ground beef, lamb or veal balls, steamed*
sole or salmon bits* (bone-free), (eeek again, fish sticks are popular),
French toast*
hard boiled or scrambled eggs*
any fruit, (banana, pear chunks, peach, strawberries, mango, etc.)
halved seedless grapes, halved raisins
avocado pieces
bean curd cubes
mung bean sprouts,
lightly cooked zucchini, carrot, bean, beet, snap peas, squash cubes,
    sweet potato, chopped swiss chard, broccoli flowers
bread in any form, and
cool noodles in any form, chopped

Dizzying, isn't it? I wish I ate like this. Toddlers may eat like horses until they're about two and a half, when they became suspicious of practically everything. This is a standard ploy.

Egg Custard

Preheat the oven to 325°F.

2 cups of milk
¼ cup of sugar (4 tablespoons)
4 egg yolks
½ teaspoon of vanilla extract

Beat all this together and pour into four little ovenproof cups and put the cups in a pan of hot water in the oven for an hour or less. To test for doneness, slide a knife in near the edge of the cup. If the blade comes out clean, the custard will be solid all the way through when cooled. Chill the custards for at least two hours. If you don't have twins, or if your child won't want custard four days in a row, halve the recipe.

Rice Pudding

An excellent thing to do with leftover rice.

1 cup of cooked basmati rice
2½ cups of milk or 2 cups of soya milk and 1 cup of water
3 or 4 cardamom pods
½ teaspoon of ground cinnamon
2 or 3 tablespoons of dried sweetened coconut
1 tablespoon of brown sugar

Mix all this together in a small saucepan, cover, and simmer gently for a half hour or until most of the milk is absorbed by the rice. Press the rice with a spoon to thicken the texture. Remove the cardamom before serving.

Hummos

Big time protein.

½ cup of dry chick peas or a tin, ready to go
1½ cups of water
a bay leaf
juice of a lemon
2 teaspoons of ground cumin
3 tablespoons of tahini (ground sesame seeds, check your local grocery store)
2 tablespoons of sunflower seed oil or another oil
salt to taste

Put the chick peas and the bay leaf in a saucepan with the water, cover the pan and bring the water to a boil. Turn off the heat and let rest for a half hour. This brings the peas to the same point they'd be if you'd soaked them overnight.

Check that the peas are still covered with water. Turn on the heat again and simmer them gently, covered, for 45 minutes or until they're really tender.

Chick peas are called *ceci* in Italy and *pois chiches* in France. You could be thinking about this while you boil them. You could think about the protein of legumes, the fat-freedom, the clean good taste. You could also read a good book during this interval. To your child.

Or, skip this part by opening a tin of chick peas and rinsing them very well.

Remove the bay leaf and purée the chick peas in a food processor with as much cooking liquid or additional water as is needed to make a smooth paste. Add the lemon juice, cumin, tahini, oil and salt, and serve it to your child on whole wheat pita bread pieces or toast.

Also great with pita chips or vegetables dipped into it, or spread on focaccia and topped with grilled eggplant slices. The first time I had it was in Tel Aviv in 1969. It had gorgeous olive oil drizzled on top, and we ate it with skewers of barbecued goat, olives and big pieces of crusty bread. Whew.

Pancakes

This makes three or four nice ones.

1 egg
½ cup of unbleached flour, less 1 tablespoon
2 tablespoons of wheat germ
½ cup of milk (soya milk tastes very nice*)
½ teaspoon of baking powder
pinch of salt
1 tablespoon of melted butter or oil, plus more later

*Soya milk is thicker than cow's milk, and you need to dilute it just a bit. Put ⅓ cup soya milk in your measuring cup and fill with water to the half-cup mark.

In a bowl, beat the egg with a whisk. Add the flour, baking powder, wheat germ, milk and salt, and mix well. Melt butter in a little frypan for individual pancakes. You could make three or four pancakes at once in a larger pan if you wanted to. Kids like towers of small pancakes very well.

Pour the melted butter into the pancake batter and mix it through.

Then pour a circle of batter into the frypan and cook over medium high heat until bubbles appear all over the surface, then flip it over and fry a minute or two longer. Cook all the pancakes this way. Put a little more butter or oil in the pan for each one. Serve with maple syrup or corn syrup or apple sauce, or stewed plums, or a blob of yogourt.

Our daughter Emma sometimes mashes a ripe banana and adds it to the batter. This makes a delicious pancake that is crispy and sweet. Or you can add fresh blueberries or strawberries to the pancake as it lies in the pan, placing whole or sliced (respectively) fresh fruit on the uncooked side before you flip. A tablespoon of sunflower seeds or walnuts is also very nice, if your child has molars.

Crêpes

This recipe is enough for two 2-6 year olds, about 6 large crêpes.

two eggs
½ cup of unbleached flour
1 tablespoon of wheat germ
½ cup of milk or if soya milk plus 2 tablespoons of water

Whisk this together vigorously. If you are using soya milk, it is creamier than good old 2% and you'll need to add a tablespoon or two of water to thin the batter.

Heat your favourite frying pan. Non-stick pans are good here, but gramma's good old cast iron pan works very well also. Or you may be among the very lucky who have a real crêpe pan, which works best of all. Just preheat the pan, this is important, and for the first crêpe, spread a hint of oil or butter in there. Butter will burn, so don't put it in until you're ready to go. You may not need any more lubricating once the pan is really hot.

With the handle of the pan in one hand and your wrist limbered up, pour some batter at the edge of the pan, rotating the pan so that the batter slides around the whole flat surface. Use a circular motion here. The quantity of batter that you pour depends on how large the pan is. You want a thin layer all over the bottom of the pan, and any excess that is sloshing about, you can dump back into the batter bowl.

If your crêpe is rather thick, as in pancake, add more milk or water. This takes some practice, and there really isn't any other way to tell you how to do it. It's one of those things, like roller blading or playing pool, that you get better at eventually, and is very satisfying.

Anyway, when you see the edges of your crêpe are browning, flip it over for a short fry on the other side. Then place it on a plate, sprinkle on some lemon juice and a little sugar, or orange juice and sugar, or spread with cream cheese, or maybe your child will like a little cocoa powder and sugar and cinnamon, or sliced bananas or peaches fried in butter. Do what you will, but roll it up in a cylinder and offer it to your gaffer.

Keep on frying until you have used up your batter. Leftovers, if any, can be nuked, or you can use them to make *crêpes suzette*, should you get the urge, or blintzes (recipe below).

Blintzes

Ideally, double this recipe and freeze half the blintzes for another day. Fry frozen blintzes without thawing.

1 recipe of crêpe batter (above)

Filling:
½ cup of cream cheese
½ cup of ricotta or cottage cheese
grated peel of half a lemon
1 teaspoon of lemon juice
2 teaspoons of sugar
1 egg yolk

Mix the filling ingredients together in a bowl. Make your crêpes as before but cook them on one side only, stacking them fried side up. Use a small (6") pan to make the crêpes.

When all the crêpe batter is used up, assess your filling to determine how much to put into each crêpe. Got eight crêpes? Divide filling into eight and put that blob onto the middle of the topmost crêpe. Fold up the bottom onto the filling, the left side, the right, the top, a nice firm envelope. Put your blintz aside, and fill the next one the same way.

You can now freeze them, or put them back in the pan, fold-over side down, and fry in butter, turn once, until brown on both sides.

Serve with sour cream, yogourt, apple sauce etc., whatever your child loves.

Applesauce

Could hardly be easier. Nice organic apples, like macintosh, empire or ida red. Wash 'em, peel 'em, cut 'em up, removing seeds and stem, put in a saucepan with a tablespoon of water and bring to the boil. Cover tightly, turn the heat to low and simmer gently until soft, maybe 5 minutes. Then stir vigorously. Jar, refrigerate, eat soon, or freeze for later.

Whole Sautéed Chicken Livers

I love to eat liver, but it's the one thing I feel guilty about eating. It's the organ that cleans the blood, after all, so that all the growth hormones and antibiotics that are fed to sad boxed-up chickens have got to be in there, don't they?

So! At least, let's get organic free-range chicken livers, so that the horrid stuff is confined to the odd bug the chicken picked up while walking around in the barnyard.

Wash the little livers and cut off any fat. Fry them gently in the oil of your choice, or butter, until browned on the outside and not too pink (just a tiny bit) on the inside, about 10 minutes, while stirring now and then. You can also steam them, for five minutes, for more fat freedom. Salt lightly, maybe. Let cool a bit and hand one over to your toddler. Think about what a wonderful source of iron liver is.

Steamed Meatballs

Not going for fancy here, just nourishment. Get the ground meat, whether chicken, pork, beef, veal or combo thereof. Add nothing, except maybe a tiny sprinkle of soya sauce. Bread crumbs are good too, as they make the meat ball less sturdy. This is a good thing.

In a bowl, mix whatever you're using with the meat, and roll it into balls about one inch in diameter. Set them into your handy steamer and let 'er rip until the balls, when pressed, feel firm, maybe 8 minutes. Cool a bit, serve. Or freeze, for quick nuking some other day.

French Toast

1 slice of whole wheat bread
1 egg
1 tablespoon of milk or soya milk, or water
Or, 1 egg yolk and 2 tablespoons of milk. (Some kids like this better because there are no egg-white filaments, which can look pretty freaky on your toast. The oddest things can be scary-looking.)

Whisk together milk and egg in a shallow bowl. Dip the bread in, and flip it over right away. All the liquid will be absorbed while you leave it lying there.

Heat a frypan and add some butter. Fry the bread until brown on each side. Serve with maple syrup, ideally. Other things are also great: apple sauce or corn syrup, blueberry jam or plum preserve.

Eggs

My gramma told me what to do to get a nice hard-boiled egg. You put the egg in cool salted water in a saucepan over medium heat. Salt makes the cooked eggs easier to peel. The water comes gently to a boil, and the shell doesn't crack because the temperature change has been gradual. Boil the egg five minutes, she said, and then take it out of the water, crack the shell, and refrigerate it. This has worked for me.

Sometimes I serve the egg right away: peeled, in a cup, with a little salt and pepper, and a tiny dot of butter chopped into it. Kids who like eggs like this.

Scrambled egg is a question of familiarity. Actually, most things are a question of familiarity. Have you ever been to another country with your small child? Nothing tastes right to her, it's not quite the same. Sometimes kids eat nothing whatsoever while on vacation. The upside of this situation is that they don't get dysentery.

However, we're on the pattern-setting mode here. An egg that has been well beaten, then spilled into a small frypan in melted butter and left undisturbed until mostly set, flipped for hardly any time at all and served, has been very popular with us. A little sea salt or Kikkoman (or other light soy sauce), as we always point out, is optional.

Brown rice fried with egg

This is another good use for leftover rice. Gently fry cooked rice in a pan with a little oil or butter, stirring from time to time. When the rice is warmed through, add a beaten egg and move that around until it's blobby and not too runny, a minute or two should be enough. Sprinkle on a few drops of light soya sauce and serve.

Sole or Salmon bits

Or any other fish of your choice. Just get all the bones out—be really careful about that part.

Steam, or fry gently in butter or oil, until firm to the touch and flaking (3 or 4 minutes for sole, and for salmon it will depend on the thickness of the piece). Add nothing. A squirt of lemon juice, if you feel you must. It's vitamin C, after all. Check for bones again. Serve small chunks and feel happy about great minerals and easily digested protein. They call this Brain Food.

Lightly cooked vegetables

The wonderful things that you did with vegetables from your garden or market for puréed baby food, you can now duplicate without the purée part. You get the freshest, most vibrant looking beauties each day or two, and you chop and steam them for a few minutes until they can be chomped without difficulty. Zucchini doesn't take long (two minutes), carrots take longer (six).

I hope this will not offend, but you can see in your child's diaper if the veggies you have cooked are soft enough to digest, and you adjust accordingly. If there are big blobs of carrot in there, well, cook your carrots longer. You want the veggies to be accessible nutrition, but without leaving all the food value in the cooking water.

You know by now which vegetables your child likes. Some babies will try anything and some hate absolutely everything. Oh well, we keep trying things. Or, we don't give up puréed veggies until high school. Whatever it takes, it doesn't matter.

Don't forget to save the vegetable cooking water for soup stock.

Yogourt Shake

Whatever it is that you serve to your squirt, you lay down a precedent for future eating. So you want to provide a broad spectrum, as it were, lots of choice and experience. Somewhere in the twos, everything loses favour, because kids stop growing as rapidly, and they require less calorie input. So they get choosy, and that's okay.

With us, yogourt shakes stayed popular through thick and thin.

1 cup of yogourt
a peeled banana
a half cup of hulled strawberries or another colour of fruit
(ripe pear, peeled mango)
a half cup of orange (or apple or other flavour of) juice
whirled together in the blender, served for breakfast with some
toast (wheat or rye) on the side.

This is the Recipes for a Small Planet approach: the combined elements that produce protein, in this case grain and dairy. Yogourt is okay for some lactose intolerances, otherwise use a square of tofu in your blender, gloriously benign and flavourless and packed with protein.

The precedent that was set with these shakes, for our teens, was an evolution to the JUICER. Without batting an eye there are, these days, carrots juiced with fresh ginger, apple, beet and a few drops of echinacea, or soya milk with almond butter and dates. Eeek. Very serious nutrition.

Meat need not figure in our lives, as everyone knows. Protein powder is a nice alternative in the shakes. Foods combine to make protein, like grain and legume (noodles and lentils), or dairy and grain (cheese on toast, or milk and cereal), though dairy doesn't agree with everyone. There's a new tofu powder, which is a wonderful convenience food. It comes sweetened, and you can use it instead of milk. My sister gets it in her health food store in Whitehorse, Yukon, but not every town has it.

Tips for the Non-Consumers

Some kids eat heartily and some don't, and there can be any number of reasons for it. If your child is restless in the highchair, you can try placing a selection of items on a plate, handy, while the child wanders and grazes, selecting what she wants and eating while otherwise absorbed. Table manners can come later.

Kids love to cook. Sometimes, when they won't eat, this sort of subversion may do the trick. They like to help make their own sandwiches, spread the butter and slap on their own tuna salad. Or go all out and do open-face, with do-dads and dingle-dangles on it to make faces or monsters or animals. Alfalfa sprouts for hair, red pepper lips, carrot noses, zucchini ears. Silly is good. Julienne of dried apricot moustache. Whatever. Hijiki seaweed skirts.

You make a little fuss. Together, write down the recipe for the completed dish, or draw it, or take a picture of it. There! You made something, and that was fun. And then you have to back off, don't you. No guilt trip: "We went to all this trouble and now you won't even eat it?!" Nope, like that he won't.

We've heard moms say so many times: the more trouble you go to to make something for your child, the less likely it is that he or she will eat it. In fact, it's a Law.

Or there's this one: "I just leave Bobby alone with his lunch and he eats it right up." Or not! We felt so smart when our girls would eat lasagna; later, our boy wouldn't eat a thing. Who can say? The lesson learned is that parenting is accommodation. Everybody's different and everybody deserves an opinion.

Little kids like to dress up. They like sing-songs and goofy fingerplays, and bumpy games where they slip gently off your lap, and rhyming games where they count their ears, and tickling games, and the slippy colours of fingerpaint. Food is goofy also. Heaven knows there's enough time to get heavy about things later on.

Some kids eat heartily and some do not

CHAPTER TWO

The first time we had little buddies over from school, I prepared by cooking all morning. I fixed a vegetable platter including carrot sticks, cherry tomatoes and raw cauliflower, a fruit salad with kiwi and grapes and nectarines, a green leafy salad, and sandwiches: egg salad, tuna salad and ham and swiss, all on whole wheat bread. I set the table and made little place cards, set everything down in the middle and drove off to school to pick up the kids.

Boy. They were not thrilled; in fact, they were intimidated. Five little girls came in happy and skipping and halted at the table, mute. They had in mind something a whole lot more low-key. Actually, it was the playing they had counted on. Food was just what took away the pain in their stomachs so they could get on with the fun.

Little kids don't like too much choice. They don't like unfamiliarity. Life has too many surprises as it is. For instance, you look down and suddenly your T-shirt is on backward. How did that happen? Or you look really closely, but "M" and "W" look exactly alike. It's so confusing.

The little girls at this lunch didn't know what half the stuff on the table was. They didn't like the brown bread, they didn't want green leaves, they couldn't read the place cards. Also I'd overlooked that four-year-olds have appetites like birds. Everyone would have been perfectly happy with peanut butter on Wonder bread, a slice of apple and a cup of juice. I'm just the friend's mom, not the dietitian, not the food educator.

So they ate practically nothing. After a while, to break the tension, they began a prim little foodfight. They were, after all, ladies.

If I had set it up differently, there might have been a hope of success. If we'd talked in the car about what they would find at our home, had I asked if they liked tuna or egg salad, they would have had some time to think it over. Or if I'd suggested that they get the dress-up clothes out first and pretend they were at a fancy party, they'd have had a chance to get in the mood. But they still probably wouldn't have eaten anything.

Now when kids come over, lunch takes five minutes and then off they go to play. They really only want to see the other guy's toys, anyway. Exploration of the new house may take an hour or so, and then they'll come to see what else you've got going.

Kids love repetition. It gives them a feeling of mastery. Very often, they'll ask for the same lunch every time they come. It's what they know, and it saves time.

Crafts

Are similar. If you do plaster of paris molds with them one day, they'll ask for that again next time. This is a good project for multiple visits anyway, since you have to let it dry overnight and paint some other day. Never pick a complex craft on a first visit, like stuffing and sewing together a little doll, because when they ask for it again you'll want to jump out the window.

Puzzles are nice to do together, for a break, if the kids are running around a lot, but they have to be quick puzzles, the 24 or 36-piece size.

Booklets are quite popular. You staple a few blank pages inside construction paper covers and provide decorations for the outside with any supplies you have: stickers, sequins, buttons, bits of cloth or paper or cutout magazine pictures. I used to routinely cut up magazines as I read them, saving any interesting pictures for the cut-and-paste supply. The kids make their drawings on the pages inside, whatever the theme might be, like Easter bunnies or Halloween monsters or kids swimming. That's good for at least half an hour.

One more craft involves cheap cotton gloves for everyone. You also need dollmaking supplies like curly hair, googly eyes, odd shapes of felt for tiny shirts and pants, and white glue. On each of the four fingers of the glove you make a little person, a character in the latest favourite nursery rhyme. Goldilocks and the Three Bears. Little Red Riding Hood (wolf, gramma, woodcutter). The Three Little Pigs and Wolf. Then you have a visual accompaniment to your storytelling, in these little finger puppets.

Also great for lootbags at birthday parties. You can send everyone home with a little art supply kit, to work on at home. You rescript the old tales, follow the example of the rewrite on Jack and the Beanstalk

(Jim and the Beanstalk*), wherein Jack is sympathetic to the lonely Giant, and the Giant is grateful. Try the Three Little Pigs of the Future. Little Red in the Nineties. We're all good storytellers.

But this is a cookbook, and we like baking with kids. There are some wonderfully illustrated kids' cookbooks that we have covered liberally and frequently with cake batter, but you don't even need one. Any recipe can be fun, if you just let the kids help.

*by Raymond Briggs

Two children can work on a baking project quite well if the tasks are parcelled out. One child does the wet ingredients: the eggs, butter or margarine, vanilla, peanut butter, carrots. This is the *Wet Person*. The other is the *Dry Person*, handling the flour and getting the thrill of measuring spoons for baking soda, powder, salt, cinnamon and whatnot. The beater gets heavy to hold up, but luckily at about the same time that everything is blended together. Kids can spoon out cookies, and each person gets to lick something, a spoon or a nearly empty bowl. And then at snack time, whoopee! And everyone has a fruit or a carrot alongside.

Brownies

The Wet Person does this part.

Into a bowl, measure:

½ cup of butter, or margarine, or soya margarine, and beat it with
1 cup of sugar until it's even textured. Then beat in the contents of
2 eggs

The Dry Person does this part:

Measure into a bowl:

½ cup of all-purpose flour or spelt flour*
½ cup of cocoa
½ teaspoon of salt

Dump all the dry ingredients above into a sieve suspended over the butter mixture. Sifting is a lot of fun, and you have to try to get most of it into the bowl. Finally, you beat the wet and the dry together, and the beater makes a little cloud of flour and cocoa over the bowl that you don't breathe too deeply.

Someone could be moving a little butter around in an 8-inch square cake pan, perhaps the Wet Person.

Now someone muscular plops the whole thing into the 8-inch square pan and smooths it down. Kids may decorate the top with walnuts or almonds.

Bake at 350°F for 20 minutes or until the top looks dry and the brownies' edges are shrinking slightly away from the sides of the pan.

*Spelt is wheat, but it's such a primitive and distant cousin that for most people with wheat allergies, it can be safely substituted, and in equal portions to all-purpose flour.

Peanut Butter Cookies

The Dry Person can start things off by attempting to measure:
1 cup of peanut butter. Luckily, any approximation will do.

The Wet Person gets the next part.
Measure:
½ cup of brown sugar, squashed down. Pour over it
½ cup of white sugar. Dump this into a bowl.

Add:
½ cup of soft butter or soya margarine and beat them together.

Then add:
1 egg and
½ teaspoon of vanilla and beat again.
This child could now get out the cookie sheets.

The Dry Person, fresh off peanut butter, gets the next part.
Measure:
1½ cups of all purpose flour or spelt flour
½ teaspoon of salt
½ teaspoon of baking soda, and stir these together.

Add the peanut butter to the sugar/butter mixture. Beat gently to blend. Then add the flour mixture. The result is fairly stiff.

Both kids can roll the dough in their hands into little balls that are each about the same size (smaller than ping pong balls) and put them on the cookie sheet. (Grease the tin if you feel you have to.)

The kids must press gently with a fork (dipping the fork first in water helps) on each little ball to flatten it just a bit. Bake the cookies (there'll be about two dozen) for 15 minutes at 375°F, but watch them, because the bottoms can burn.

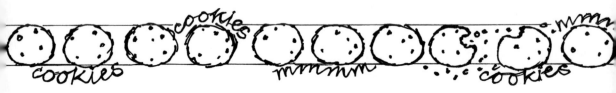

Carrot Cake

This makes a LOT of carrot cake.

Use a bundt pan or a 9 x 13 inch flat pan, or make four little 4 x 8 loaves.

The Wet Person measures into a large bowl:

1½ cups of oil (sunflower seed oil is nice) and adds
4 eggs, then beats these two together.

Next there's the carrot preparation for the Wet Person to do, peeling and grating, without including knuckle skin. You want

2 cups of grated carrot

Just take your time and sing something soothing.

Meanwhile, the Dry Person swings in with:

2 cups of sugar, added to the oil/eggs, all of which is then beaten together until smooth. Stop the beater and measure the following together in another bowl:

2 cups of all-purpose flour or spelt flour
1 teaspoon of cinnamon
2 teaspoons of baking soda
1 teaspoon of baking powder
1 teaspoon of salt

Stir these around. Then add half the mixture to the bowl of wet stuff. Beat gently and then put the beater aside. With a big spoon, stir in the grated carrot.

Ask the Wet Person to drain:

1 small tin of crushed pineapple. Add it to the batter. The drained pineapple juice may be drunk by all, on the spot.

Ask the Dry Person to add the rest of the flour mixture and stir.

Nuts and raisins can go into this mess, if you like, half a cup (or more) of each. Somebody has to grease the cake pan.

Pour the batter into the bundt pan and bake at 350°F for an hour, or into the 9 x 13 pan and bake for 35 or 40 minutes, or until a toothpick comes out clean, or until the edges are brown and lifting slightly from the pan.

This is a gorgeous cake, moist and rich. It keeps well for close to a week, or it freezes, and you can serve it plain or put a lemon icing on it. We have baked it for years, and the kids say, each time it comes out, "GREAT CAKE!"

Zucchini Muffins

(makes 18 big muffins)

One person washes the zucchini and trims off the two ends. You need:

2 cups of grated zucchini, which in summer is something to do with those zucchini zodiacs that take over your garden.

Wet Person beats:

3 eggs with
¾ cup of melted butter (or oil) and then adds
1½ cups of sugar and
1 tablespoon of vanilla. Beat this all together, then relax.

Meanwhile the Dry Person measures:

3 cups of flour
1½ teaspoons of of salt
½ teaspoon of baking powder
1 teaspoon of baking soda
1 teaspoon of cinnamon

Now, combine the grated zucchini, the wet stuff and the dry. Stir around with a big spoon and it will be quite stiff. You can add chopped walnuts or filberts if you are keen. Kids can spoon this into muffin papers in your muffin tins, or the whole mess can also be dumped into a breadloaf pan, and just baked longer. Muffins take 20 minutes, or until brown and the toothpick comes out clean. The loaf takes an hour, or more, both at 350°F.

Cathie's Fabulous Chocolate Zucchini Cake

Another truly great thing to do with zucchinis.

In a large bowl, the Wet Person creams together:

¾ cup of soft butter or margarine or soya margarine
2 cups of sugar
and when it's nicely beaten and light coloured, add
3 eggs and beat well. Then add
2½ teaspoons of grated orange rind
2 teaspoons of vanilla
2 cups of grated zucchini
Mix this with a wooden spoon until blended homogeneously. (This mixture usually curdles at this point, which looks really weird, but the curdles disappear in the final product.)

Meanwhile, in another bowl, the Dry Person combines:
2½ cups of flour
½ cup of cocoa (sifted)
2½ teaspoons of baking powder
1½ teaspoons of baking soda
1 teaspoon of salt
1 teaspoon of cinnamon
Now, combine the wet and dry. This is best done by dumping half of the dry stuff into the wet stuff bowl, mixing gently with a spoon, and then sloshing in
½ cup of milk, stirring gently
Then add the rest of the dry stuff, and stir gently again.

This beautiful moist cake can be baked in a 9 x 13 pan, and frosted when cool with your favourite chocolate icing. For this approach, you pour the batter into the aforementioned 9 x 13 greased pan and bake at 350ºF for 35 or 40 minutes. Do the toothpick thing to be sure.

Or you can bake this in a greased bundt pan, in a 350ºF oven for more like an hour. To finish it, in a bowl, make a sauce from:

¼ cup of icing sugar
1 tablespoon of orange juice
½ teaspoon of orange rind
Pour over the decanted, warm chocolate cake.

Delicious either way.

Big Chocolate Cake

This cake deserves a Hall of Fame award. It's hard to mess it up, it makes a lot of cake, it's moist, delicious and dark. Great for school parties, since it's good for over a dozen little kids. I copied this recipe from a Hershey's cocoa box twenty years ago and have made it fifty times.

In a large bowl, the Dry Person combines:

2 cups of white sugar
1¼ cups of flour
¾ cup of cocoa (you gotta sift this)
2 teaspoons of baking soda
1 teaspoon of baking powder
½ teaspoon of salt
Stir this around gently as long as you want.

In another bowl, the Wet Person combines:

2 eggs
½ cup of oil
1 teaspoon of vanilla

Then decide among three possible approaches, all equally good.
Either
2 cups of buttermilk
or
1 cup of buttermilk and 1 cup of strong decaffeinated coffee
or
1 cup of yogourt and 1 cup of coffee (my favourite)
Beat all of the above together with a whisk or a beater.

Add the wet to the dry and beat again just until smooth, not much. Whoever isn't doing the beating can oil a bundt pan to bake this in.

When ready, pour the batter into the oiled bundt pan and bake at 350°F for 40 to 45 minutes, or until a toothpick comes out clean.

Let the cake cool for 20 minutes or so and then reverse the bundt pan onto a suitable cakeplate. Sometimes you have to slide a thin rubber spatula down the sides to help the cake release from the pan. When the cake is cool, sieve some icing sugar over top for decoration and it will look very sophisticated.

For Christmas put tinsel on the edge of the plate, at Halloween put orange jellybeans in the hollow centre, and for Easter use foil-wrapped chocolate eggs and those pieces of plastic straw that you see everywhere.

Fruit Preserves and Warm Semolina

Ideally, use prune plums. Their tart skins and sweet flesh combine when cooked to produce something astonishingly good. Rhubarb has the same appeal. Semolina, a cereal, is made of finely ground wheat. Check the dry food section in any food store.

For the plums:
2 pounds of ripe prune plums, split in half and pitted
¼ to ½ cup of sugar
pinch of cinnamon
1 tablespoon of water

Put these together in a saucepan, and then put over low heat, covered, and simmer for twenty minutes, or until the plums are nice and sloppy.

Or you could use rhubarb instead of plums:
5 cups of rhubarb stems, coarsely chopped
1 cup of sugar
½ cup of water or orange juice

Place together in a saucepan, bring to the boil, and simmer gently for 5 minutes or until soft.

For the semolina, figure:
a quarter cup of dry semolina for each person having some

Sprinkle the dry grain into four times as much boiling water while whisking, and stir over low heat until the cereal is thickened, which might be about five minutes. Sweeten if you like. Serve in bowls with the cold preserve on top. Hot/cold, tangy/sweet, really an amazing dessert. This is Mme Hélène Menth's recipe, the very kind woman who looked after her family and her farm and everything else at my *pension* in Switzerland when I was seventeen. You should taste her homemade sausages, with melting leeks, potatoes and mustard, or her perfect gruyère fondue (for this latter, see page 139). I hope to have another dance with her by her living room radio some day.

This is a great dessert for kids, soft, delicious and good for them. My daughter insisted on it being included in this collection.

Variations:

You can make a double recipe and put the plums in jars. (They will keep for a week or two in the fridge.) I certainly would. They're fantastically delicious on toast for breakfast. Or you can use them to make a nice tart, slide them cut side up onto a sweetened half-baked flan shell, add some cooking juice and lemon zest and bake until bubbly. This is a very nice pie. Or use them on top of sweetened cream cheese or lemon curd in a baked flan shell for a cold tart.

They're just too yummy to do only one thing with.

Lunch for the Small Set

Getting back to those kindergarten kids: what do they eat, in the successful scenario?

Well, you ask them what they want. Sometimes they'll say white bread and peanut butter. Sometimes they'll hold forth on animal rights.

Cow's milk/wheat allergy kids do pretty well with goat cheese melted on rye toast. Try lentil soup or chicken stock with nice vegetables floating around in it, or just good old Campbell's chicken noodle. Vegan kids are often familiar with miso soup. If your child has a vegan buddy or is lactose/wheat intolerant, you will know that there are clean (meaning wheat/meat/additive/lactose-free) dry-packaged soups in huge variety in health food stores, a couple of which you can just have on hand for when that child is over. A little 100% rye bread in the freezer and boom, you're ready.

Some kids live on bagels, cream cheese, breads and spreads, and dips and raw vegetable sticks. Pita bread toasted in triangle shape, dipped into hummos, or topped with melted cheddar or egg salad, goes over pretty well. Many kids like comfort foods like macaroni and cheese, tuna noodle casserole, pastas, peanut butter spread into celery stalks or rolled into iceberg lettuce leaves.

Non-spicy casseroles, like chili made from tinned beans, perhaps served with corn bread, can fill a vegetarian bill in a hearty way. In this age group, the 3 to 8 year-old set, peaceful food is most appreciated. These recipes can be found below.

When our oldest kids, the twins, were two years old, I scolded the kindly cornerstore owner for giving them candy. I wanted their nutrition to be perfect. I've mellowed. Snacks that kids love include toast that is buttered and then sprinkled with cinnamon and sugar, or apple slices that are treated the same way. This is an effective diversion for the kid who won't eat a plain apple. Whatever. Would we really rather that the child had nothing? Tough call, I guess.

Tuna Casserole
(microwave!)

2 cups of elbow macaroni (wheat or quinoa or buckwheat)
4 cups of boiling water
1 can of tuna
1 can of condensed mushroom soup
½ cup of mayo
1 teaspoon of worcestershire sauce
½ teaspoon of celery seed
1 teaspoon of black pepper
1 cup of assorted diced vegetables which could include all or a combination of green pepper, red pepper, green onion, frozen peas or anything else that you have in your fridge.

Topping:
½ cup of grated cheese (like parmesan or romano or pecorino)
½ cup of bread crumbs or crumbled cornflakes

Cook macaroni in boiling water for 7 minutes.
Meanwhile in a medium casserole, combine the contents of the tuna and soup tins with the rest of the ingredients.

Add cooked macaroni, mix, and sprinkle on the topping. Place in microwaveable casserole and cover. Serve, or chill until needed.

To serve later, bring to room temperature, and then nuke for ten minutes on HIGH. Or warm in conventional cookware, in conventional oven, at 350ºF for 30 minutes, *comme vous voulez.* If the latter, it's a good idea to remove the cover for the last 10 minutes in the hope that the topping would get crispy.

Macaroni and Cheese

3 tablespoons of butter
3 tablespoons of flour
2 cups of milk
1 cup of grated cheddar
1 cup of dry elbow macaroni
salt and pepper

Boil the macaroni in lots of salted water, stirring occasionally.

Meanwhile, melt the butter in a large saucepan, and then stir in the flour. Stir with a whisk, and cook for 2 minutes over medium heat. Add milk, stirring, until the sauce starts to thicken. Add grated cheese and stir while it melts. Check the seasoning, and add salt and pepper if you want to.

When the pasta is cooked (7 minutes or so), drain it into a colander and then dump the noodles into the cheese sauce. Stir and serve.

Tinned Chili

2 tablespoons of vegetable oil
1 heaping tablespoon each of chili powder and ground cumin
½ teaspoon of chili flakes (optional)
1 clove of garlic, minced
1 diced onion
1 diced celery stalk
½ each of diced green and red pepper
1 can of baked beans
1 can of kidney beans, drained and rinsed
1 can of crushed tomatoes
1 bay leaf

Heat the oil and add the seasonings and vegetables. Stir and fry for about 5 minutes. Reduce heat, add the tinned foods and the bay leaf and simmer gently, stirring occasionally, for about a half hour.

CHAPTER THREE

Every Place Takes Two Hours

All of my best childhood memories are beach picnics. I'm a fool for a beach. I have endeavoured to instill this fanaticism in my children, and it's worked fairly well. We live in Toronto and that is the geographical base for this section. I wish I were picnicing in Victoria, or Halifax, or Regina, or Wawa, or Brandon, or Whitehorse, or some of the other places I have loved to visit. However, you know your cities better than I, and you know how to have a good time.

You don't have to plan for weeks. Many towns, like ones in southern Ontario, make a real point of being great for picnics, providing fried perch or pickerel so good that they knock your socks off. Some coleslaw, some fries, some seagulls and sun, you're there.

Northern Ontario picnic spots provide thrilling water and wind, trees that point east, big fish, astonishing air, pink rocks, blueberries and, if you're lucky, loons singing down the sun.

What you need for these B.Y.O.s is your trusty cooler and ice packs. You bring juice boxes or recycled water bottles with juice in them that you can have right away, and others that you froze last night full of water or lemonade or Koolaid, that gradually thaw out, there on the beach, or in the canoe, that you drink later in the afternoon, or even on the drive home. You make great sandwiches at home, wrap them individually: bun, lettuce, mayo, sliced turkey, pepper, cheese, whatever. It's easier to make them at home because you don't have to remember to bring knives and mayo, and it's faster when everyone is hungry. You must have nectarines and grapes, these are essential, or pears and watermelon, those may be essential also. This is electrifying food when you really need it, sitting on the granite slopes of the French River, the wind in your hair, the lead in your pencil.

The main thing is to get outside. Everyone brings a hat. You must also have sun block, a wet rag in a plastic bag for tidying up, some towels, and your swim suit. You may decide that you, the parents, are allowed a beady cup of cold white wine. You may bring an extra towel for the dog.

Whether spending the day at Science North in Sudbury, or dropping kids off at camp in Minden, relaxing by the Irondale rapids (the picnic spot on Hwy 503 out of Kinmount), admiring the fields of lupins near Picton, or running in the windswept beaches at Sandbanks Provincial Park, you never know, you might see a good-looking lake and want to stop for a swim, and pick fireweed, and have your picnic right there.

Vanilla Mocha Peach Lime Lemon
Strawberry Pineapple Raspberry Chocolate Neapolitan

The Beach at Port Dover

At Port Dover on Lake Erie there is a great small fishing town. Less than two hours from Toronto by car, take Hwy 6 southwest from Hamilton and bring your blanket and the big beach umbrella.

THE ARBOUR has been at the main intersection forever. They serve fantastic burgers, dogs and fries. Their claim to fame is the drink they serve, in many flavours, named the Glow. Peach Glow is our favourite.

Parking is a pain, but you may get lucky with street meters, or unload everything at the beach and then go off a couple of blocks to the parking lot.

Immediately landward of the beach is one of the world's best fry stands, KNETCHEL'S, where you purchase clam strips, shrimp in a basket, dazzling fresh-caught crunchy fried perch and other fishes, and perfect coleslaw. There is also a salad bar. This you carry with you to the sand, where the water is divine for little guys, since it goes on being shallow practically forever, you can walk fifty feet before it's waist deep, amid bobbing water toys. Very rarely, the wind stirs up enough wave activity for body-surfing. We have swum in this lake for 50 years: it's getting cleaner all the time.

There's a GREAT ice cream stop on the way home: HEWITT'S, on the south side of Hwy. #6, near Hagersville. They even make yummy goatsmilk ice cream in several flavours.

The Beach at Sauble Beach

   Sauble Beach is a lovely resort town at the base of the Bruce
Penninsula, Lake Huron side. There are orchards and farmlands,
great lakefish and grazing cattle, loamy earth and market gardens.
Food stores sell fresh caught pickerel, salmon trout, angus beef, field
corn, perfect tomatoes and crisp apples. The beach is wind-blown,
with sand dunes and elegant long-stemmed beachgrass. Rent a
cottage here and be happy as a clam all summer. Take bicycle trips up
the Bruce Trail. Visit beautiful Meaford, on the far side of Owen
Sound, on Nottawasaga Bay.
   To visit Sauble Beach, it takes about two hours. Go to Owen
Sound, through Guelph north on Hwy. 6, through picturesque
rolling farmland. Turn northwest up Hwy 70 through Shallow Lake,
cross Hwy. 6 through Hepworth, and you're there.
   There are lots and lots of beach cottages for rent all along the
lakefront. Enjoy the produce. Bring your hibachi.

Grilled Splake (Salmon Trout)
with coriander lime butter

Brush off your grill thoroughly and oil the splake fillet well on the skin side. Mix together:

2 tablespoons each of ground cumin,
ground coriander and
brown sugar with
1 teaspoon each of salt and pepper

This dry mix you push onto the flesh side of your fish filet.
Put the filet flesh side down, ON GREASED FOIL, on the grill of your white-hot barbecue. Cover if your barbecue has a cover. After 4 minutes you cleverly flip the foil over, placing the oiled skin side of the fish down on the bare grill, and cook 3 more minutes.
The fish may be done now or not quite, depending on the thickness of the filet, the heat of the fire, the set of your jaw. You watch, and if you open it up a bit with a fork and it looks raw, leave it longer. "Done" is still juicy, but delicately flakey and opaque right through the fish.

Coriander Lime Butter or millions of other butters

tarragon and lemon
parsley and garlic
feta and rosemary
sage leaves and shallot

Chop finely a handful of carefully rinsed fresh coriander leaves and add the grated skin of a nice lime. Squeeze and add the lime juice.

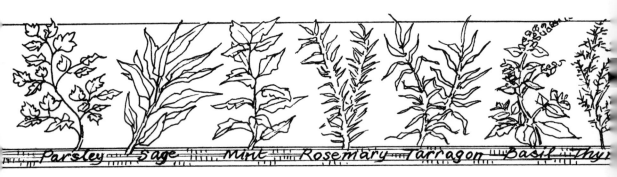

Parsley   Sage   Mint   Rosemary   Tarragon   Basil   Thyr

Stir this all into ½ cup of soft butter, and lay the butter in a sausage shape on waxed paper, adroitly covering and rolling the butter in the paper. Refrigerate until firm. When ready to serve, unwrap, and slice into ¼ inch rounds. Put one on a hot cooked fish (or chicken or beef or pork or tofu) serving and let it melt luxuriously.

Do tarragon and lemon exactly the same way. If you don't have fresh tarragon, use a tablespoon of dried. Great on a fish, eggs or cornmeal-coated, fried tomatoes.

One clove of garlic may be enough for the parsley and garlic idea, or you may like more. Serve on a baked potato, steamed green beans or beef filet.

Cream the feta with the butter when you do that one, crush the rosemary into it, and serve it on a lamb or pork chop.

Chop the shallot finely with the sage leaves and butter. Serve it on butternut squash or pork roast.

You could serve any of them on any pasta.

Pepper is always a good idea, so I would add it lavishly to any of these combinations. My sister says: always use a heavy hand with spices, "unless, you know, it's ketchup or something."

The Beach at Sibbald Point

This is a provincial park on Lake Simcoe, with a nice camp ground. Great for birthday parties for 6 to 11 year-olds, it has a big beach and a huge playground, and it's the closest access to large clean water from Toronto. It's LESS than two hours by a long shot.

From Toronto, go straight up Hwy 404, to Newmarket, cut east on sideroad #31 to #48, where you turn left, north. You'll see Provincial Park signs in 20 minutes, just past the turnoff for Sutton. You can make it in one hour.

Set up your teepee for the weekend or just spend the day. Bring food. Bring lots of drinks. You can buy wood or bring your Coleman stove. The kids will leave you alone all day, playing in the windy, sparkling water.

There's an entrance fee per van. You drive in and follow the signs to the beach parking lot. You can get pretty close, and parking is free.

Birthday Party at Sibbald

For six small kids, in your cooler you put:

18 juice boxes, half of them frozen the night before.
12 hot dog buns
12 hot dogs
carrot, cucumber, celery sticks, radishes, etc. (washed, in a plastic tub)

Not in the cooler are:

relish, ketchup, mustard
A boiling pot, the coleman stove, fuel, tongs. The nearby campground has water faucets.
(Alternatively: charcoal and starter fluid and the hibachi, because they don't have barbecues there)
a watermelon, and a really big knife to cut it
8 plates
a roll of paper towels
a few small knives for condiments
parents' favourite drinks and food (I don't like hot dogs)

Now, you may think of a great way to transport cake and ice cream, but I don't know one. I would serve them when we get home later, and have the birthday present opening then too.

There aren't many bugs to deal with at Sibbald, because of the wind off the water, but there are bees and seagulls. You can do a bit of a nature walk, see fish in the weeds to the east of the beach, and, if you're desperate, there's a snackbar on the west side

Bronte Creek Provincial Park

Bronte Provincial Park is the only prairie grass preserve in Ontario, and it is habitat for creatures unique to the province. Naturally, it is in danger of being redeveloped as a golf course. This would be really stupid.

It's southwest of Toronto along the Queen Elizabeth Way, and it also has the biggest wading pool in the known galaxy. It costs extra to use it, but it may be worth it. There's a petting zoo and the best barn of all time, with slides, fling-yourself-off-the-precipice-to-the-landing-cushions, swash-buckling rope swings, and all-round great play. You sit quietly outside the barn, waiting for your child to tire. It's not two hours away, either; it's closer.

You get your entrance to the park per van, and then you drive all the way around to park (free) WAY over in the southeast corner of the park. There is a snack bar there, actually, there's a burger place, but feh, you bring the cooler and the terrific lunch.

First you go to the wading pool/lake, where there are 7 lifeguards and a sandy play area for little guys and great fooling around swimming. You can relax on the grassy hills around the pool, bring your beach blanket. When it gets really hot and sunny, go back to the car and get lunch out, and after you've eaten, there's an ice cream stand.

After that, drive to the barn. It's near the main entrance. (You may not want to do all this driving, you may have brought your bikes and want to tour around that way. Older kids may even want to sight-see the wonders of this ecological miracle. I'm only thinking of the cooler and not wanting to drag it around.)

Vanilla Mocha Peach Lime Lemon
Strawberry Pineapple Raspberry Chocolate Neapolitan

Picnic at Bronte

Also a great place for a birthday party, though more expensive than Sibbald.

For six little kids, into your cooler you put:

  18 juice boxes, half of which you froze last night
  10 sandwiches, buns or bread, lettuce, mayo, whatever
  Ham and Swiss? Tuna salad?
  Cheddar and pear? Chicken and apple? Peanut butter and jam?

  Find out if someone has an allergy; otherwise, give a choice of two
sandwiches. Too much choice makes for conflict.

  tomato & cuke slices, celery and carrot sticks in a sealed plastic tub
  2 extra buns for the person who wants nothing else
  cantaloupe with a knife to cut it

Not in the cooler are:

6 chocolate bars for dessert, and
2 big bags of potato chips or popcorn for the drive home.
2 litres of water or Koolaid, previously frozen, and cups...

Later, they'll be thirsty.

❖   ❖   ◆

The French River (or any canoeing picnic)

Assuming this is a short trip, not the days on the river with a different campsite every night, the reflector oven to bake your bread, the soups on the coals, the chappatis in the frying pan, 2 pounds of oatmeal for breakfast. On such a trip you would be thinking energy food, juice, dried fruits, nuts, power bars, pasta, rice and lentils, hot chocolate and teas.

No, this is the nice little day on the water, lily dipping with the cooler full of great stuff, no fire, no tent, no fishing lines. For this picnic you need something rustic and cultural, something reflecting the unbelievable beauty through which you are travelling, suitable for the moment when you pull your canoe up onto pink granite and remove all your clothes in order to have this little moment with the sun, wind, rock and sky.

For two canoes, in your cooler you pack:

Wild and Brown Rice Salad

½ cup of raw wild rice
½ cup of raw brown rice
¼ cup of wheat berries
½ cup of shelled pecans
2 oranges, peeled and sliced
1 handful of chopped fresh parsley
Dressing: ½ cup of sunflower seed oil
              3 tablespoons of Kikkoman (or another light soya sauce)
              a few drops of sesame seed oil
              ground black pepper to taste

Rinse rices and wheat berries, drain and cook in 2½ cups water until tender, about 45 minutes. The wild rice splits and makes lovely little curls. Let cool.

Pop the pecans on a tray in the toaster oven and toast as for a slice of light toast. Let cool. Combine in a mixing bowl the rice, cubed oranges, parsley and nuts.

Whisk together the dressing ingredients and pour over the rice. Stir to mix and store covered in a cool place. The Bamboo Club on Queen Street in Toronto is a cool place, you could try that.

Ginger Carrots

6 or 7 slender carrots, grated coarsely
1 inch cube of peeled fresh ginger, grated finely
½ cup of dried apricots, chopped
1 clove of garlic minced
¼ cup of canola oil
juice of 1 lemon
salt and black pepper at will
Combine ingredients and let the flavours integrate in a covered container.

Tourtière with Chicken and Mushrooms

Pastry

2 cups of unbleached flour
1 cup of shorteningor ½ cup of Crisco and ½ cup of margarine
1 egg
1 tablespoon of white vinegar
2 tablespoons of water
½ teaspoon of salt

This is the recipe off the shortening box. It makes a nice flaky crust. For a sturdier crust, substitute ½ cup Lactancia margarine or another soya margarine for half the shortening. This crust travels better, but take your pick. Chop together the shortening and flour until the texture is grainy. Add the other stuff, stir together. Take a break. When the dough has rested, about 15 minutes, divide it into two equal balls and roll each one out between opened up plastic bags that you have recycled from the supermarket, in which you brought home your apples or lettuce. This way you don't need to add more flour, and clean-up is a snap.

Lay one of the pie crusts in the bottom of a nice flat 10" flan pan.

Filling

1 pound of ground chicken
½ cup of bread crumbs
2 beaten eggs (optionally reserve 1 tablespoon aside—see below)
12 fresh white mushrooms, sliced
½ Spanish onion, chopped
2 cloves of garlic, minced
½ teaspoon of dried rosemary
½ cup of chopped fresh parsley
1 teaspoon each of salt and pepper

In a little olive oil, fry the sliced mushrooms over medium high heat until they are browning on both sides. Add the onion and cook until soft, about 3 more minutes. Add the garlic and stir in the rosemary. Dump all this out into a bowl.

In this same pan, put the ground chicken, and fry for 3 or 4 minutes. Turn and let it brown on the other side. Begin chopping the mass up into little chunks. We need not have this chicken totally cooked, because it's going into the oven, but we want to get it well on its way. Add the chicken to the bowl with the mushrooms and add the parsley, the beaten egg, salt, pepper, and breadcrumbs. Add about a ¼ cup of water to the frypan you have just emptied, and scrape up the brown stuff off the bottom of the pan. Pour this into the bowl with everything else and stir.

Pour this mixture onto the piecrust in the flan pan. Place the other rolled pastry on top, and seal the edges decoratively. If you want to be very fancy, brush the top with the reserved beaten egg, and bake at 350°F for 30 to 35 minutes or until the crust is golden. Cool and then chill.

When you're ready for your picnic, pack the bowls and the pie in the cooler and go. You need plates, forks, napkins, dijon mustard and a pie knife for the tourtière, as well as fruit for dessert in case there are no blueberries at your campsite.

The Grand Boat Picnic

Ever go on a sailing cruise? Land at a beach, anchor out, build a fire, cook up a bouillabaisse? Not impossible. On the boat-trip to the beach, the kids troll. Sunfish won't do, throw them back, but perch are great, and obviously if you are lucky and get bass or pickerel you are a better man than I. Gut 'em, scale 'em. Perch stay whole and larger fish can be beheaded and then chopped in two.

Freshwater Fish Soup

(for six people)
In advance at home, prepare and seal in a plastic bag together:

a fennel bulb, and an onion, chopped
5 or 6 cloves of garlic, peeled and halved
1 or 2 leeks well washed, white half only, chopped
4 carrots, peeled and chopped
3 stalks of celery, chopped coarsely.

Separately, chop 2 cups of fresh tomatoes and a big handful of rinsed fresh parsley. Pop these into a yogourt container or seal in a plastic bag.

Bring wood for the fire, or bring the Coleman stove, whatever. Bring a big pot, and clean water.

At the campsite, get your fire going.

In your big pot over the wood fire or Coleman flame, fry the vegetables gently in olive oil with 3 bay leaves until wilted.

Add 8 cups water, cover, and bring to a boil. Simmer 5 minutes, and then add:

a teaspoon of saffron threads
2 cups of chopped tomatoes (prepared at home)
½ cup of fresh chopped parsley (same)
the cleaned fishes and fish pieces
salt and pepper to taste

Bring back to the simmer and cook gently, stirring now and then, for 10 minutes, or until the carrots are tender. Taste, correct for salt. If you haven't caught any fish, you still have a very nice vegetable soup.

Ideally, with this you have Pernod, the French pastis apéritif. You need a good crusty bread to dip into the soup. A few dried chilies sprinkled in doesn't hurt anyone. You also need cold canteloupe and lime wedges to squeeze on them for dessert. A really great summer day is tremendously advantageous.

Near an ocean? Snapper are ideal, or any non-oily fish at hand. Add any shellfish that you find. Throw in a crab, lobster, clams, whatever. Urchins should be eaten raw. Wear a hat.

Other Ideas

Indoor Picnics

Most of the recipes mentioned here are in this cookbook.

We pretend to be Swiss, and have fondue or raclette, before the wood fire, with boiled potatoes, mustard and cornichons.

We pretend to be Italian and have antipasti, pizza, lasagna, and luscious bagna cauda.

We pretend to be Mid Eastern and have cushions on the living room floor, eat couscous, hummos and shashlik, olives, flatbread, harissa and chickpea soup. Camels can stay outside.

We pretend to be Guadeloupian and have stuffed blue crabs, fishes fried in coconut oil, spicy chicken with bananas, and then bananas flambéed in rum. We all wear bathing suits.

We pretend to be Japanese and have miso soup, tempura, some sushi maki, tiny bits of marinated grilled salmon, steamed rice. Refined outfits. Swanning about in kimonos.

We pretend to be Vietnamese and drink pho, the gorgeous beef breakfast soup, and eat fresh spring rolls and peanut sauce, smoky eggplant with lime sauce, and make sticky rice. For this we need palm fronds.

We pretend to be Greek and have grilled squid, moussaka,

taramasalata, tzatziki, skordalia, olives, pita and feta. BBQ'd racks of lamb would be nice too, eh? Then we all say OPA! as we light the saganaki.

We pretend to be Indian and have bharta, goat curry, tandouri chicken, spiced basmati rice, naan, pickles and chutneys.

We pretend to be New Englanders and have a fine Seafood Boil, with shrimp and mussels and root vegetables, drained and poured out onto newspaper to eat with the hands.

Here follow a few suggestions:

The Swiss Picnic

I have actually had a Swiss picnic. I'm an incredibly lucky person. Picture the surrounding mountains, the azure sky, the dense chocolate colour of the wooden chalet and the red geraniums on the balconies. Now see the red checked tablecloth on the picnic table, the earthenware jugs of light red wine, the platters of salami and pasta and spicy pickles and fruit. You're in the shade of the grape arbor, so you don't get sunstroke. You're in the Italian part of Switzerland, so there's no one in *Lederhosen*, but you may supply an accordion if you wish.

But our party is an indoor picnic. Traditionally, for this we have the roaring fireplace and a rack to hold the half wheel of raclette cheese close enough to the heat that the exposed side melts. With a knife, you deftly swipe the melted cheese down off the wheel onto a plate, and eat it with boiled potatoes, pickled onions, lots of dijon mustard, and black pepper. Seriously delicious.

The sensible way to go about this with little kids is to choose a milder cheese, like cheddar, since raclette is fabulously stinky, and repels small children in droves. Use the toaster oven to melt it. Costumes may take on an important role: go for the newspaper caps with little feathers sticking up, and maybe knee socks, shorts and suspenders.

Serve pea soup and call it Potage St. Germain. Small boiled potatoes are the way to go, with slices of cheddar melted in the toaster oven on little trays of foil and slipped off onto the plate for each person. Sweet gherkins are popular with kids, and regular dill pickles are fine too. Swiss chocolate bars for dessert, or be very exciting and melt some in a little pot and let the kids dip strawberries, grapes or melon. *Et voilà*, a chocolate fondue.

The Italian Picnic

The picnic I'm thinking of has the warm smell of the ocean blowing in the wide open windows, at mid-day in August with the cicadias singing. To start there's homemade pizza, and lovely antipasti like pickled vegetables, happy cubes of mozzarella cheese with crusty Italian bread and olives, melon and salami. The second course is a spaghetti, and there's red snapper in wine sauce that precedes the veal, porcini and cream entrée. Afterwards everyone enjoys a little cappucino and sherbet, says "buon giorno" and tips over for a nice long nap.

For the kids, we can make lasagna. Pop Pavarotti on the player, serve grape juice, discuss the comparative virtues of Ferraris and Lamborghinis.

Lasagna

My pan is 10 x 15 inches, fits the recipe below, and serves 10 to 12 people. Since lasagna freezes beautifully, make lots and be all set for some other day.

Sauce
3 tablespoons of olive oil
1 Spanish onion, chopped finely
4 cloves of garlic, chopped finely
5 roma (plum) tomatoes, trimmed and chopped coarsely
1/2 cup of fresh parsley, chopped finely
2 cups of crushed tomatoes (a big tin)
2 cups of prepared spaghetti sauce
salt and pepper

White sauce
2 tablespoons of olive oil
1 tablespoon of butter
3 tablespoons of flour
1½ cups of milk
salt and pepper

Filling
2 cups of ricotta cheese
½ cup of plain yogourt
1 pound of fresh spinach, trimmed
1 egg

Pasta
15 strips of dry lasagna noodles
1½ cups of grated mozzarella cheese
¼ cup of grated parmesan

Start boiling water for the pasta. You need a really large potful of salted water. Wash and trim the stems off the spinach and plunge the leaves in this boiling water for 15 seconds, just to wilt it. Pluck it out and set aside to drain. Now boil the pasta until just done, about 6 minutes, stirring frequently. Drain and let sit in cold water until needed.

Make the tomato sauce by frying the onion in the olive oil over medium heat until it begins to colour, about 10 minutes. Add the other ingredients, cover and cook gently 20 minutes more, stirring from time to time.

For the white sauce, melt the butter in the olive oil and stir in the flour. When bubbly, whisk in the milk and cook until thickened. Season to taste. Pour this into the bottom of the lasagna pan and tilt the pan to coat the bottom evenly.

Squeeze the water out of the spinach and, in a bowl, add it to the ricotta, yogourt and beaten egg. Stir until blended.

Now you're ready to assemble the lasagna.

Lay five strips of cooked pasta side by side atop the white sauce in the lasagna pan.

Spoon half the tomato sauce on the pasta and spread it evenly around, covering the pasta completely.

Lay five more strips of pasta on that, and put the ricotta mixture on top of them. Spread that around so that the thickness is uniform, and cover the ricotta with another (final) layer of pasta.

Dump the rest of the tomato sauce on top, and sprinkle both cheeses evenly over the surface.

Cover with foil and bake in a preheated 350ºF oven for an hour, or until the cheese at the centre of the pan is completely melted. Let it sit for 10 minutes before serving.

CHAPTER FOUR

Parties Without Agony

Birthday parties are nice, but kids will celebrate at the drop of a hat, and certain special occasions deserve theme parties. Some that are particularly popular are the following:

the We're Done with Diapers party, or
the Superb Report Card party, or
the You Graduated From Nursery School party,
the Wart Is Gone party, (or the Cast Is Off),
the Welcome Back From Camp party,
the Some Kinda Fabulous Stitches In Your Knee party, or
the You Made the Swim Team party (or Volleyball,
Baseball, Hockey, Basketball, Part In The Play, etc.,
endlessly).

These are usually family-only parties, since the topics are personal: people are a bit embarrassed by diapers by the time they are done with them. But they are opportunities for intrepid interior decoration and seemly foods.

At this Diaper Party, for example, older siblings can reminisce, smaller ones can look forward with pride, single ones could invite a bosom buddy or two. Everyone would in fact wear a diaper, over the clothes, and at some glorious moment, fling it off. Walls and plant-life could be festooned with appropriate paraphenalia, like suckers and nursing bottles and stuff that exaggerates the passage out of baby-dom and into kid-dom. There should be a cake (appropriately decorated with dopey stuff), perhaps a small keepsake present (NOT a bronzed diaper) and dancing.

In summer, waterguns are a nice touch, boinging in the back yard; in winter, perhaps the Mummy-in-Toiletpaper game would be easier on the upholstery. You play this game by dividing the party into teams of two. One member of the team is wrapped in toilet paper by the other member. You need fairly good quality toilet paper, or else it keeps tearing in the most frustrating way. The room gets absolutely covered in paper, which pleases the smaller people very much right away: the mayhem aspect. There's also the thrill of competition. The winner is either the first team all covered, or the most imaginative covering, whatever is decided beforehand. And there may be a prize, like a temporary tattoo or a tiny action figure or a Barbie sweater or a sesame snap.

Nursery school graduation, that's easy. Gotta have the square black board hat with the little tassle dingle dangling, and a circle of cardboard inside to hold it on the head. Gotta have the cake, the rolled-up diploma, invite gramma and grampa, put opera on the record player. Cucumber sandwiches are *rawther* nice, if your child doesn't mind, and action snapshots are necessary. Speeches should be kept to a time limit.

Seasonal parties are also cinchy, like a Halloween party. Your child invites friends home after school on Halloween night. You have decorated with black and orange streamers, the jack-o'-lantern is on the dinner table with candles lit, the drapes are drawn and have little witches and pumpkins pinned all over them. Kids spend half their time getting their costumes just right, then your pizza arrives. Serve a float of green sherbet in ginger ale for a ghoulish effect and BLOOD oranges. Cranberry juice is nasty too.

Try Dodging for Donuts (donuts suspended by strings, kids' hands behind the backs), or Pin the Wart on the Witch (child chews up bubblegum, is blindfolded and approximates the location of the witch's nose on a poster-sized drawing). Then you have the little talk about street safety and go out trick-or-treating for a half hour or so. Count kids regularly. Get the parents to pick up their ghouls around 7.30 pm.

Hundreds of ways to dress up and all over the place to go.

CHAPTER FIVE

While in hospital delivering our third child, I had as a room-mate a person as prepared for motherhood as Watson was for Holmes' extrasensory conclusions. Less, actually. The young woman had no visitors, she was lonely, she spoke little, she kept trying to call her mom back home overseas, she had a huge episiotomy that hurt her. She was miserable. She had a huge, bawling, robust baby, lying on the bed beside her where the nurse had laid him, crying and thrashing in his little blanket, hungry. And she rolled her eyes at me, bewildered, anguished and clueless as to what she could do.

Has this ever happened to you? Unexpected, eh? That nature would leave you so high and dry? She usually provides so well for these situations.

Pregnancy, for instance. Why is it nine months long? It's to give you time to get used to the idea. To teach you how to walk more slowly, to get your head out of the workplace and into looser wardrobes, healthier foods, home-ier activities. To get you used to waking up a few times each night, changing your perspective about goals, having less control over everything in general. To get you in the mood.

Gently but relentlessly pregnancy rolls you along from hormone to hormone, in a rhythmic and predicted template: THIS is the WAY women have DONE this for THOUSANDS of YEARS.

And childbirth, there's another good example of the power, the grand design of existence, how your body takes over its task, at a time of its choosing, uncontrollably, superb in intent, and terrific in irrepressibility. Fantastic. So you would think nursing would be as undeniable.

To my room-mate, I suggested, as you might have done if you'd been there, that she let her baby put his little lips on her nipple. Great idea! Babies are born with few predeterminations, but among them is an instinct for sucking. No problem on his end. And a nice hospital case worker moved in for the next few days to guide us over other rough spots.

Any number of things could clog the great design. Maybe you only get six weeks maternity leave. Or your nipples crack, and nursing is just too painful. Or you have to be separated from your newborn early on, for whatever reason, and your milk never gets established. There are so many ways nowadays that a perfectly good biological system can get waylaid.

Breast feeding is not only the most nutritious and all-round beneficial thing you can do for your baby, it's also the most convenient and satisfying for both of you. But sometimes even perseverance doesn't work.

Sometimes women don't have any luck with breast-feeding, and they feel like heels. This is silly. Whatever works, works. It's the contact that's important, not the vessel.

Margaret Ribble's wonderful book, *Rights of Infants*, calls mothering the most indispensable ingredient to infant development, "the warm, indulgent and consistent support of parents to a small organism who is assumed to have no racial memory, and absolutely no ability or idea of how to adjust to life."

Ribble calls the mouth the first sense organ. Sucking helps respiration and blood circulation, it's relaxing and provides security.

The top of the head is also sensitive, such that head-stroking and bodily massage actually give the infant life.

It also develops her self-awareness. The baby feels her body. She's new in town, doesn't know anybody but you, and, well, you want to show her a good time. You help her out each time she calls. She's incapable of evaluation, so the reliability of your response to her allows her to learn what cause and effect are, and encourages her efforts (which are reaching, focussing, recognition and vocalizing) to bring about desired reactions. Contact is a protection, a stimulation, an education and a comfort.

> Human milk is the food perfectly adapted to the human infant. Colostrum, ringing with antibodies from the mother's immune system, is produced in the breast at childbirth. Milk production is stimulated by the infant's sucking, and milk arrives two to four days after the baby. This gives everyone time to get acquainted. You know you're doing the right thing, so you just give your child a nipple anytime she wants it.

About eleven o'clock at night in the second week, you'd like to hang your breasts up in the closet and give them a nice rest. They're sore! They're swollen up, and there's someone pulling away on them all the time. AAGHH!

Of course, you have to offer a bottle early on anyway, or a cup, for extra fluids. In summer, babies need water. And when you want to go out, the sitter can offer something that isn't too weird. Possibly you might express breast milk and freeze it, so the sitter can warm it up on these occasions, and serve from the bottle. Also, maybe your child will permit a dummy, a suse, a placebo (whatever you call those nipple things without a bottle attached), which is wonderfully handy during teething times. My kids would never take one.

Some foods that you eat turn up in your milk to give your baby gas, and you may have to give up things like brussels sprouts. This is sacrifice.

Sometimes women have great luck. My friend successfully breast-fed her twin boys, and I suspect others have done it too. It wasn't as cozy for her: as they grew stronger, the boys would kick each other over her stomach, and she was restrained by their number, in that

with two hands and two breasts and two boys, she didn't do much else at mealtime but sit there with her shirt open. But it worked. She had enough milk, the boys got big, she didn't get too rundown, they had good peaceful times together, nursing. And it didn't last forever.

With my own tiny (premature) twins, I was encouraged by my pediatrician to give supplemental bottles of formula, so that we had all of the aggravation from both avenues. We had to boil bottles and buy cases of formula at midnight, and my breasts leaked milk that slipped down my shirt any time I was out without children. The first month's schedule was something that would be outlawed by the Geneva Convention.

A sample from their log shows that in 24 hours, there were 8 hours of actual eating, in 16 separate feedings. I wish I had tried to give one baby the breast exclusively one day, and the other just the bottle, and switched them the next day. Or that I had tried to go with just the breast. Or whatever. I wish I had tried things. We were new parents and didn't feel confident. My husband and I were so tired after a few months of this, I was so tired, that my milk supply drifted away. I would forget to offer the breast. They were gaining weight well and were happy with the formula. And bingo, they were weaned.

Time goes by, and your child doubles his size. He can sit up, he has opinions, knows where his toes are. Here's a guy ready for pablum.

With our third child, I was so darned happy with breast-feeding her that I forgot to do the pablum thing. One day she plucked a chicken drumstick off my dinner plate and started to chew on it.

We wised up fast. For us, Milupa was first, which we moistened in a bowl with expressed breast milk, and kept warm in a surrounding bath of water. She sprayed it experimentally sometimes but mostly seemed hungry, and interested, which is why we started giving it to her in the first place. At the end of the day, there didn't seem to be enough breastmilk to satisfy her, she wanted something more.

Following the pablum inclusion, she gained weight, mainly cheeks.

At seven months, we began adding cow's milk to my expressed milk to make pablum, in order to make more pablum without squeezing myself all morning. She took half a cooked eggyolk mashed into it for breakfast, strained meat and vegetables at lunch, more pablum and fruit at dinner. The world exploded. Organic vegetables of any kind, stuff from my garden, steamed briefly, buzzed in the food processor, served. Two minutes, bingo. Add a blob of tofu, and that covered protein. Homemade applesauce! Fresh squeezed oranges! And stuff saved, individual servings frozen in ice cube trays, as autumn came on.

But she wasn't the eater in our family. She was curious and accepting but there were lots of things she'd fling across the room rather than let them touch her lips. Everybody's different.

Amusing to read Spock, the definitive standard for Boomers, who said six-month-old kids are likely getting cereal, egg yolk and 6 ounces of milk from a cup for breakfast. His lunch and dinner are also pretty hilarious. At this age, my first-born children drank four or five ounces from their formula bottles and went back to sleep.

They gathered momentum slowly, however, and eventually got tall and graduated from high school. Childraising, or rather, living with children, is a process, during which you just try to keep your eyes open and think on your feet.

CHAPTER SIX

Way Before High School

The tender years are over. After kids finish grade two, the world is their oyster. Goodbye to worries over counting by twos or by fives, they've got that licked. Hello to reading, writing, multiplication, team sports and bosom buddies.

Kids eight- to twelve-years-old take challenge on the chin, they can manage more by themselves, and they want to. They're rambunctious, opinionated and frisky. If they start by trying new foods, they'll end up by inventing their own. By the time puberty slams 'em, they've had a pretty good time.

These are kids who can enjoy new shapes of pasta and new sauces. They'll give eggs another whirl, whether scrambled, poached, or fried. They'll brave granola, tofu, layered sandwiches, new soups, and seasoned meats and vegetables, stir-fries and casseroles. In other words, without giving up old standbys and comfort foods, they'll explore taste.

In this chapter you will find:

1. *Soups, quite a few*
2. *Things to Do with Tortillas*
3. *Things to Do with Pita Bread*
4. *Interesting Low-Key Casseroles*

1. *Soups*

Miso

A great source of protein and minerals.

2 lengths of kombu seaweed (dried)
7 dried shiitake mushrooms
4 slim carrots
1 pound of tofu
½ cup of brown rice miso, or another light coloured miso
2 green onions

Peel the carrots if you want to, and slice them quite thinly. Put them in your large soup pot, add 8 cups of water and bring it to boil for 3 or 4 minutes. Take the pot off the heat and put the kombu in there to let it steep, like tea, for a half hour. Remove the kombu. (There are recipes for pickled kombu, if you are keen, but so far I just pitch it out.)

Meanwhile, steep the mushrooms in boiled water to cover, in a bowl, for the same time interval. When they are soft, trim off and discard the tough stems and slice the mushroom caps in 5 or 8 pieces, depending on their size. Save the soaking water. Strain it through a fine sieve, and add it to the soup pot.

Rinse and drain the tofu, and cut it into small cubes. Chop the green onion into slivers.

Put the miso into a sieve and lower the bottom of the sieve into the soup. Swish, stir, let sit, stir again. When you remove the sieve, you want the chunky miso parts to be all that remains therein.

Put the pot back on low heat, add the tofu to the soup, and warm through. Garnish with the green onion. This soup is delicious and extremely nutritious for any age group.

Pea Soup with a Ham Bone

Start with Beautiful Ham Stock. This is how you make it:

Use your mostly denuded hambone leftover from the Sunday roast. Place it in a stock pot with any bits of ham no one wanted to eat. Wash well and don't peel the following: a medium onion, 2 ribs of celery, 3 hefty carrots, 2 cloves garlic, and a fistful of parsley stems. Chop this all quite finely, without killing yourself. The onion skin gives colour to the stock as well as flavour, but use only one skin, because they can be bitter.

If you have leftover leek leaves, wilted celery tops, slightly tired raw squash, this sort of thing, add it too. Not brassicas. I feel cabbage, broccoli, brussels sprouts, Chinese mustard greens, bok choy, etc., all develop a tinny taste in stock.

Add water to cover the vegetables and bone. Add 2 or 3 bay leaves, a big pinch of rosemary, about a dozen peppercorns, and no salt. Bring to a boil, turn down the heat, and let simmer gently, half covered, for a couple hours. This makes a fantastically good stock.

Strain the stock and throw out the solids. Clean the pot and add a little olive oil. Fry in this oil a peeled, chopped half-onion, a few carrots, peeled and chopped into engaging shapes, and two washed and cubed raw potatoes. Stir. Add a cup of dried green split peas and a half cup of red lentils if you like them. Stir and add your Beautiful Ham Stock. If you don't have six cups of liquid, add enough water. Stir and let cook gently until the peas are soft, an hour or more. Mash the vegetables with a potato masher, just a few strokes to break up the peas. Optionally, add finely chopped cabbage or Swiss chard greens for the last ten minutes before serving. Check for salt and add it if you want to.

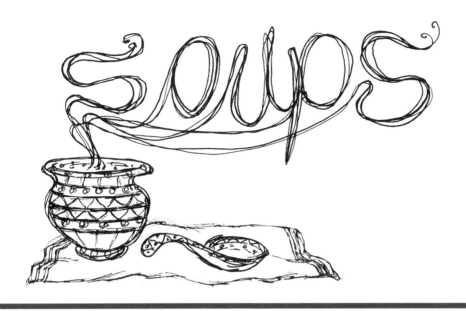

Pea Soup (Vegetarian)

1 cup of dried split green peas
1 small onion, 1 medium carrot, and 1 small potato, chopped
1 tablespoon of soya sauce or miso paste
2 teaspoons of black pepper
1 teaspoon each of dried basil and thyme

Place split peas in a sieve and rinse well under cold running water, thcn add to a pot containing 4 cups of cold water. Add chopped onion, carrot and spud.

Add soya sauce and remaining ingredients and heat to almost boiling, without ever actually letting it boil for any length of time or you'll find the peas sticking to the bottom and burning. It's best just to have the soup seriously simmering for approximately an hour, or until the peas have softened.

This is a beautiful soup and perfect for kids this age. It can be changed if you feel you must: use the snazzy vegetarian soup stocks available, or plain vegetable stock in bouillon cube, after checking the additives.

Vegetable Stock

Vegetable stock is sort of a state of mind. I have a drawer in my refrigerator which gradually collects things that will be good for vegetable stock, and when a critical mass is reached, I boil them all gently together for a half hour with enough filtered water to cover, a few bay leaves, some peppercorns, red chili flakes, and sometimes tomato paste or a few dry mushrooms. This makes lovely stock for any vegetarian soup or stew, and the house smells wonderful.

The kind of things to save up are wilted carrots, parsnips, tomatoes and celery, that outside layer of onion, sprouting garlic cloves, leek greens, chard stems, corn cobs, squash peels and seeds, and herb stems, especially parsley. Don't use anything slimy, of course, but think of it as a sort of special class of vegetable: too good for compost, not good enough to serve as is.

Don't save brassicas. I don't save them, anyway. If you want cabbage, broccoli, rapini, collard or brussels sprout soup, add it to your unadulterated vegetable stock. Once I made stock with the skins of about twenty onions and oh, it was awful.

Strain your stock, season with salt, and use in place of chicken stock anytime you want to.

Tom Yam Soup

1 large cube of firm tofu cut into little cubes
1 cup of Chinese dried mushrooms steeped in boiled water for 20 minutes
3 tom yam cubes *
6 cups of water
1 tin of bamboo shoots, rinsed and chopped
1 inch cube of fresh ginger, peeled and finely sliced
1 cup of frozen peas
2 tablespoons of cornstarch mixed in ¼ cup of cold water
garnish with sesame oil, green onion and a beaten egg

Boil the water and dissolve the tom yam cubes. Trim the stems off the mushrooms, slice them thinly, and add them to the broth as it heats. Add the ginger and cook gently for 10 minutes. Add the cubed tofu, the bamboo shoots, the peas, and warm through. Stir in the cornstarch and let heat thoroughly. Stir in the beaten egg and a few drops of sesame oil. Serve garnished with chopped green onion.

Knorr tom yam cubes are available in oriental food stores. They're terrific. If you can't find them, substitute chicken or vegetable broth for the water, 2 tablespoons of rice vinegar, and ¼ teaspoon of dried red chili flakes, or more, to taste.

Red Pepper Chowder

Especially in fall, with those wonderful cheap sheppard peppers.

2 tablespoons of butter or oil
2 leeks slit lengthwise, rinsed thoroughly, and chopped fairly small (Discard the tough green tops.)
2 stalks of celery diced
2 medium Yukon gold potatoes, scrubbed and cut into small cubes
2-3 cloves of garlic, chopped finely
3 red peppers, seeded and chopped in bite-sized pieces
2 tablespoons of flour
4 cups of chicken or vegetable stock
1 cup of 18% cream or 2% milk or soya milk
1 teaspoon of dried basil
cayenne and salt and pepper to taste

Melt the butter in a large saucepan and add the leeks, celery, potatoes, garlic and peppers. Stir around over medium heat until the leeks wilt. Don't let anything get brown. Add the flour and stir it in well, then the chicken stock and seasonings. Turn heat to low, cover the pot, and let simmer gently until the potatoes are cooked, about 15 to 20 minutes.
Add the cream and check the seasoning.

Portobello Mushroom Soup
(for four to six people)

2 tablespoons of olive oil
6 smallish portobello mushrooms, dusted off, and stem end trimmed
1 vidalia onion chopped
2-4 cloves of garlic chopped
1 small potato chopped finely
splash of white wine
1 teaspoon of dried tarragon
salt and pepper to taste
4 cups of chicken stock
1 cup of light sour cream

Cook the onion and potato in the olive oil in a saucepan over
medium heat until the onion is wilted. Stir in the mushroom,
tarragon, pepper and garlic, cover and cook until the potato is soft,
maybe five minutes. Add the white wine and scrape up any little
brown bits on the bottom of the pot.

Put this into a food processor with 2 cups of the chicken stock and
buzz till smooth. Return to the saucepan, add remaining chicken
stock and bring to a gentle boil. Remove from heat, add sour cream
and stir through. Check for salt.

◆   ◆   ◆

June's Cold Curried Apple Soup

A family tradition.

¼ cup of butter
1 large onion, chopped
3 cups of chicken stock
1 tablespoon of curry powder or see recipe on page 87
2 tablespoons of corn starch
2 egg yolks
⅔ cup of heavy cream
4 Granny Smith apples (two are for garnish)
juice of ½ lemon
salt and pepper to taste
watercress leaves for garnish

Melt the butter in a saucepan and wilt the onion. Stir in the curry powder. Blend the corn starch into the chicken stock, and then add this to the pot. Add two peeled, seeded, finely chopped Granny Smith apples. Bring to a boil and cook over medium heat for about 5 minutes. Remove from heat.

Meanwhile, combine egg yolks and cream in a bowl. Add some of the hot stock to warm up the eggs, and then whisk the cream mixture into the hot stock. Cool a little longer and put the soup through a food processor in two batches. Find your nice soup tureen, pour the smooth soup therein, and chill until you are ready to serve, at least a half day, and up to 2 days.

When ready to serve, add two seeded, finely chopped Granny Smith apples, (we like the skin left on) and the lemon juice, and check the soup for salt. It will need some. Garnish with the watercress and serve elegantly on your beautiful patio.

❖　❖　❖

Henri's Garlic Soup

A very elegant soup for entertaining, this will feed 6 to 8 happy guests. The garlic, you probably know, loses its intensity in the slow cooking, and becomes just a savoury and delicious seasoning.

20 cloves of garlic, crushed, peeled, but left whole
1 Spanish onion, chopped
2 tablespoons of olive oil
2 Yukon gold potatoes, peeled and diced
10 Italian plum tomatoes, trimmed and diced
5 cups of chicken stock
a big pinch of saffron threads
a big pinch of dried thyme
½ cup of heavy cream (optional)
salt and pepper to taste

Remove the papery skins from the garlic cloves and pop them in a large saucepan with the olive oil and the onion. Cook gently until the onion is beginning to brown, about 10 minutes, stirring from time to time.

Add the plum tomatoes, yellow potatoes, saffron, thyme and a cup of the chicken stock, and let cook down for 10 more minutes. Take off the heat and cool slightly before transferring to a food processor, where you blend this delicious mess until smooth. Add more stock if you need to.

Return the purée to the saucepan, and stir in the remaining chicken stock. Bring just to the boil, and then take off the heat and add the cream, if you're using it. Check for seasoning.

Blue Crab Soup

Also great for entertaining. For 6 friends.

6 blue crabs or 2 tins salad crab meat
6 cups of chicken stock
1 cantaloupe peeled, seeded and chopped small or balled
½ teaspoon of red chili flakes optional
3 inches of fresh ginger, peeled and thinly sliced
3 green onions, trimmed and chopped
1 lime sliced, for garnish

Hit your local Asian grocery for live blue crabs. Bring them home in the paper bag and give them a snack; they like mango or banana, for instance.

Are we going to have the little talk about live food? What about that cantaloupe, humm? Doesn't she count? I think the point might be just to be grateful for what sustains our lives. Humans have to eat something, and that means some other being. If you don't want to face this issue just now, get the cans of crab instead, and the soup will be perfectly okay.

In a large saucepan or stockpot, bring the chicken stock to a gentle boil. Add the ginger and chilies, and let that steep 2 minutes.

Rinse the crabs off under running water, thank them very much for their part in your continuing nourishment, and then dive them into the soup pot, cover and cook for 4 minutes, until the shells are red. Take off the heat.

It will be easier to eat these yummy guys if you take them out of the soup and chop them in twain, bisect them, as they say in Camelot. Then you pop them back in the pot with the melon and green onions. Serve with the lime and a lot of napkins. You end up eating your crab with your fingers.

❖   ❖   ❖

Jill's Cold Cucumber and Yogourt Soup

For a hot summer night.

1 English cucumber, chopped finely
2 cups of chicken stock
2 cups of plain yogourt (Astro is so good)
¾ cup of walnuts, toasted
½ cup of fresh mint, chopped
1 teaspoon of coriander seed, freshly ground for garnish

Combine cold ingredients and serve with the coriander sprinkled on the top. Save some nice mint sprigs for garnish too. A great start to an Indian meal.

Cream of Celeriac Soup

Celeriac is also called celery root. It looks like a big ball with roots and soil all over it and tastes light and deliciously like celery. So you wash it off and peel it, then slice it up for salad. It's really nice cut in thin shoestrings with a mustardy dressing and some chopped parsley. Or you can wash and peel and cube it and boil it for soup, which is velvety and really, really good.

1 large bulb of celeriac
one sweet onion
5 cups of good chicken stock
1 cup of 18% cream
tarragon, salt and pepper to taste

Cut up the peeled root and the onion and simmer them in the stock until tender. Blenderize, add seasonings and cream, and serve.
You can also add ½ a peeled steamed squash or carrots, for variety, and a richer flavour, but you hardly need to, as it's a lovely vegetable all alone.

Lentil Soup

Serve with lemon or tzatziki.

1½ cups of dried lentils, rinsed and drained
1 medium onion, chopped
2 cloves of garlic, finely chopped
2 tablespoons of vegetable oil
2 tablespoons of curry powder *
1 tablespoon of ground cumin
1 teaspoon of dried thyme
2 tablespoons of soya sauce or miso paste
1 28-ounce can of tomatoes
4 cups of hot water
salt to taste

In a large sauce pan heat oil, then quickly add curry powder, ground cumin and thyme. Stir, and add onion and garlic, and fry, stirring, for 2 minutes.

Add the rinsed and drained lentils, and stir for a minute in order to coat lentil beans with oil.

Add hot water, canned tomatoes and their juice, and the soya sauce or miso. Bring gently to the boil and then lower the heat to simmer the soup for at least an hour. Lentils must be soft, so longer is okay.

You can use tinned lentils and save time. Rinse tinned lentils well in a sieve under running water. Cook the onions and garlic longer, about ten minutes, to soften and mellow them, before adding the lentils. Cook the soup for just a half hour, but flavours may be compromised. The soup is still good, but the dried lentils are sweeter.

*Curry powder can be bought ready made, or you can make your own. Toast in a heavy frypan: 2 tablespoons of cumin seed, 2 tablespoons of coriander seed, 2 dried red chiles, 1 tablespoon of mustard seed, and 2 pods cardamom. When aromatic, buzz it in your clean coffee grinder and in a little bowl add to it ½ teaspoon of ground cinnamon, ½ teaspoon of salt, ½ teaspoon of black pepper, 2 teaspoons of ground ginger, and 1 tablespoon of turmeric. Stir it up and store in a little jar until you want it.

Black Bean Soup

Make ham stock as above for pea soup. Vegetable stock is great too.

Wash a cup of dried black beans and put them in a small saucepan with water to cover. Add two bay leaves and bring to a boil. Reduce heat, cover and simmer until just tender, about 40 minutes. Check occasionally to see that the water still covers the beans.

In your clean soup pot add corn oil, a peeled and chopped onion and a big chopped carrot. To them add a tablespoon each of ground cumin, whole coriander seed, and peeled and chopped garlic and ginger. Add red chili flakes to taste, maybe a half teaspoon. If you are keen and you have some, a dried ancho chili or two give a wonderful smoky rich flavour to the soup without really adding much heat. Break off and discard the stem if there is one, then crumble and add the chilies. Stir, then add your cooked black beans and any liquid in their cooking pot. Pour 6 cups of Beautiful Ham Stock over top and let simmer for a half hour. Check for saltiness.

You can mash this down with a potato masher for a chunky effect, or buzz in a food processor. Buzzing makes it pretty darn thick and you may have to add more water. Serve with chopped fresh coriander leaves and blobs of yogourt or sour cream on top. Grated cheddar or monterey jack cheese is nice too.

Bean soups are great with corn bread or tzatziki.

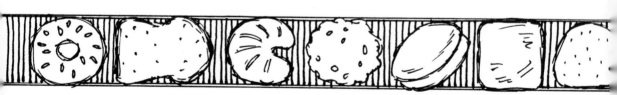

Cornbreads

Corn breads

One: you make in a bundt pan. This is light and moist.

1½ cups each of cornmeal and unbleached flour
2½ cups of milk or half milk, half yogourt
3 eggs, beaten
1 tin of creamed corn
2 cups of grated cheddar or monterey jack cheese
1 onion, chopped finely
½ cup of vegetable oil
2 tablespoons of sugar, unless you'd rather have a spicy bread. In that case, you can omit the sugar and add a teaspoon or more of dried chili flakes, or even fresh jalapeno peppers, seeded and diced.

Stir all this together and pour into the bundt pan. Bake at 375°F for 45 minutes.

Two: you make in your gramma's 10-inch cast iron frypan, if you have one. This recipe is crumbly, rich and delicious.

1 large sweet onion, a vidalia or south US sweet, chopped finely
2 jalapeno chili peppers, seeded and finely chopped
1 sweet red pepper, seeded and finely chopped
1 tablespoon of sunflower seed oil or corn oil
½ cup of corn kernels, fresh or frozen
1 cup of all purpose flour
1 cup of cornmeal
1 tablespoon each of sugar and of baking powder
½ teaspoon of salt
¼ of a cup each of shortening and soya margarine
⅔ cup of milk
1 cup of grated cheddar cheese

Fry the onion and peppers gently in your cast iron pan with the oil until they are wilted. Add the corn kernels, stir and remove the pan from the heat. Put the vegetables into a bowl and set aside.

In a large bowl, mix the flour, cornmeal, sugar, baking powder and salt. Cut in the shortening and margarine until the mixture looks like bread crumbs. This is very easy to do if you have a food processor: just put these seven things in there together and buzz for about 20 seconds. Then dump it out into a large bowl.

With a wooden spoon, stir in half the grated cheese and half the fried vegetables, and then the milk. Stir this together as quickly as you can: it's sticky. Spoon the mixture into gramma's frypan, or if you don't have one, a greased 10-inch spring-form pan.

Sprinkle the remaining vegetables and cheese on top, and bake at 425°F for 30 to 35 minutes or until just firm.

2. *Things to do with Tortillas*

Fajitas
Popular with Grades 4, 5 and 6.

1 onion, 2 stalks celery, 1 green pepper, 1 red pepper, all diced.
1 half cup of other vegetables: zucchini, green beans, whatever you like
1 small can of tomatoes, drained
2 skinless, boneless chicken breasts, cut in strips
juice of ½ lime
package of soft tortillas

Seasoning:
1 clove of garlic, minced
½ teaspoon of cinnamon
1 teaspoon of dried oregano
1 tablespoon of ground cumin
2 or 3 tablespoons of chili powder
1 teaspoon of brown sugar (optional)

In a large frypan, heat 1 tablespoon of vegetable oil over medium high heat, and add the seasonings. Stir for a minute, and add the fresh vegetables, not the tomato. Stir and let these wilt a bit, then add the chicken and stir fry, flipping everything around, for 3 to 5 minutes. You want the chicken to be firm to your probing finger, while not yet completely board solid.

Add the drained tomatoes, salt to taste, the lime juice and simmer to heat through, 2-3 minutes.

Serve in warm soft tortillas, rolled up, with yogourt on the side, or with the stiff corn packaged taco shells, with some guacamole (page 160), shredded lettuce and grated cheddar. Now it's a taco.

Falafel

What we are going for here is the glorious chick pea burger, the delightful fillings, the fab Mid-East version of the taco.

1 cup of dry chick peas
1 bay leaf

Cover dry peas in water in a saucepan with the bay leaf. Bring water to a boil. Cover pot and remove from heat for a half hour. Return to heat and cook until peas are tender, 45 minutes or so, checking occasionally that water still covers the chick peas. Drain and reserve cooking water. Place chick peas in a food processor.

1-2 cloves of garlic, minced
1 cup of chopped parsley
1 tablespoon of ground cumin
¼ cup of flour
red chili flakes, salt and pepper to taste
bread crumbs, about ½ cup

Add this to the chick peas in your food processor and buzz, with just enough cooking water to let it move around. You want this to be a thick consistency.

Make small patties with the mixture and coat with bread crumbs. Fry patties in vegetable oil until crisp on both sides.

Make your falafel by placing one or more chick pea burgers in a warmed pita pocket bread. Add tahini sauce, chopped lettuce, chopped tomatoes, chopped mint leaves, and if you like it, harissa. (See the recipe on the next page.)

◆   ◆   ◆

Harissa

A red pepper sauce, a mainstay in North Africa.

1 sweet red bell pepper or 3 dried ancho peppers
1 clove of garlic, peeled
1 tablespoon of ground cumin seed
1 tablespoon of red wine vinegar
dried red chili flakes to taste
½ teaspoon of salt
2 sundried tomatoes (optional)

If using dried chilies (slice the chili open and remove the seeds and stem) or sundried tomatoes, soak them in hot water for 20 minutes until they are pliable. Save the soaking liquid.

Place the pepper (and tomatoes) in the food processor with the other ingredients and buzz. Add soaking liquid if you need to, in order to make a smooth paste.

Check for seasoning.

Thai-Style Chicken Stuffing
(or fish or other meat)

Cut boneless chicken breast into strips and sprinkle with salt, pepper and a few red chili flakes. Broil until firm to fingertip pressure, turning once, about 3 minutes per side. Plop into a warm tortilla (there's a "Thai" flavoured one, although plain is fine) with chopped lettuce and/or coriander leaves, sliced red pepper and peanut sauce.

Peanut Sauce

½ cup of chunky peanut butter
juice of one lime
1 tablespoon of each grated ginger and chopped garlic
2 tablespoons of fish sauce
red chilies to taste
water to make a spreadable paste in the food processor

Why Not Indian? (-style Tortilla Stuffing)

On the chicken you put the chilies, salt and pepper, and a sprinkling of ground cumin and turmeric. Alternatively, equal parts of garam masala and ground cumin, used as a dredge for your chicken, give an interesting, faintly tandoori taste.

Broil away and then address your pita, adding the Indian chutney of your pleasure and some raita (page 95). Chopped lettuce is nice in there too.

Also, maybe try switching the tortilla for a pappadum (you know, the round Indian chick-pea wafers that you toast in the oven to crisp), except that they're brittle and don't roll around your stuffings satisfactorily. You have to think of them as decorative crackers. Stack up 2 or 3 and serve the chicken on top, with raita.

Quesadillas

There are people out there who routinely make their own tortillas, but I'm not one of them. I buy tortillas, sometimes wheat, maybe corn, maybe pesto, maybe "Mediterranean." There's a world of tortillas out there and by golly, they're delicious.

Quesadillas, like sandwiches, have a million ways to go. But here's a basic approach. See bottom for seriously basic, and still yummy.

6 tortillas
3 dried ancho peppers, seeded and stemmed
1 cup of grated monteray jack cheese
½ cup of dried black beans (or a tin of black beans)
2 bay leaves
½ cup of chopped fresh coriander leaves
1 tablespoon each of coriander and cumin seed, toasted and ground
1 tablespoon each of grated fresh ginger and garlic
½ white onion, chopped
½ teaspoon of red pepper flakes
1 tablespoon of corn oil (or another vegetable oil)

Bring rinsed black beans to a boil in a saucepan in water to cover with the bay leaves. Cover the pot and let simmer until beans are tender, maybe 45 minutes. Check occasionally to see that the beans are still covered by water.

Soak the ancho peppers in water to cover for ½ hour. Blend in a food processor with as much soaking liquid as is necessary to make a smooth paste. Empty into a cup, and don't wash the processor.

In a frypan, cook ginger, garlic, onion and hot pepper flakes in corn oil until soft. Add ground coriander and cumin.

In the same old chili food processor, blend the cooked black beans with the seasonings from the frypan and as much cooking water as you need to make a smooth paste.

Okay. In the same old frypan, place one tortilla. Spoon some black bean paste on top. Put another tortilla on top of that. Sprinkle on the jack cheese, and put a second tortilla on top of it.

Then, spread the last tortilla with the ancho paste, and invert it onto the tortillas in the frypan. By now the bottom is probably browning, so turn over the whole mass with a spatula, or invert onto a plate to turn. Brown on the other side until the cheese is melted and the tortilla is crisp. Cut like a pizza and serve with sour cream or guacamole.

You can get more basic. Use bottled salsa and grated cheddar. It's very good, and it's a lot handier.

Raita

Is a lovely thing and you make it (like tzatziki) by suspending plain yogourt in a clean rinsed dishcloth, in a sieve, over a bowl, for a few hours in the refrigerator.

1 cup of plain yogourt, drained
½ cup of peeled grated cucumber
1 clove of finely minced garlic
½ teaspoon each of ground pepper and cumin
1 tablespoon of chopped fresh mint leaves

Mix together and store in the fridge for up to 3 days.

Italian-Style Chicken Tortilla Stuffing

Same deal with the chicken breast, as above. Omit chili flakes and add dried basil leaves for the broiling. Brush a little olive oil on your warm tortilla (there's a "Mediterranean" flavour one) or pita pocket and fling on the cooked chicken, with chopped tomatoes and a bit of pesto.

Pesto
as we all know is

two nice handfuls of fresh clean basil leaves
¼ cup of pine nuts
1 or 2 cloves of garlic, coarsely chopped
1 teaspoon of sea salt
¼ cup of olive oil

Put all of the above in the food processor and buzz until smooth. Lots of variations are possible, like using two tablespoons of dried basil with two good handfuls of clean parsley leaves.
Here are some variations on pesto:

Variations on Pesto:

1) For a slightly Asian flavour: coriander leaves with cashew nuts, lime juice and chili flakes. Garnish your tortilla with bean sprouts.
2) Slightly Greek: sunflower seeds or pistachio nuts with fresh parsley and dried oregano. Think: feta, olives, yogourt.
3) Spinach leaves with cashew nuts, garlic and oregano. Really yummy with fried sliced mushrooms.
4) Watercress, walnuts and lemon juice, this is great on your tortilla with garlic-and-butter-fried zucchini slices, and topped with some crumbled chèvre.
5) There must be a way to make pesto with almonds, but I don't know it yet. What if it were part of a mole? A Mexican approach. Cilantro, cumin, bitter chocolate, almonds, cayenne, paprika, lime? I'm trying it tonight. I'll e-mail you.

3. *Things to do with Pita*

Pita Chips

Take store-bought pita bread and cut the flat loaves, like pies, into triangles. Separate the two crusts of the pocket and lay them out, inside side up, on a foil-lined cookie sheet. Brush the triangles with olive oil and sprinkle with dried oregano, salt and pepper, and chili flakes if you like them, or if anyone does. Toast in a hot oven (400° F) until lightly browned, about 5 minutes. Serve the chips in a basket lined with a paper towel, with a dip alongside. Hummus is particularly great, also tzadziki or guacamole dips or cream cheese, or the artichoke or caponata dips (page 160).

Pita Pizza I

In a bowl, combine:

1 chopped tomato
1 clove of minced garlic
1 tablespoon of olive oil
1 teaspoon of dried basil

Mix this around and then spread it on top of a plain pita (Greek-style is good). Sprinkle with salt, pepper and parmesan cheese. Warm in the toaster oven for 5 minutes and enjoy. A blob or two of pesto on top doesn't hurt.

Pita Pizza II

Spread attractively on your pita:

2 tablespoons of puréed roasted red pepper
2 tablespoons of crumbled chèvre

and warm in the toaster oven until heated through.

Pita Pizza III

As with Pita Pizza II, spread roasted eggplant purée on a round of pita, and top with grated provolone. Warm until cheese is melted. So yummy.

Are we wondering about these purées? Cut a fresh red pepper in half and remove the seeds. (Green pepper is good too, and cubanelles are delicious.)

Place on foil-lined tray in toaster-oven, cut side down. Turn on to broil, go away. When very smelly, check. Nice burnt skin? Great. Remove from heat, let cool, then pull off the burnt skin. Whiz in the food processor.

Eggplant takes longer. You need to cut it in half, brush on a little olive oil, and bake at 350° for a half hour, or until soft.

Take off heat and let cool. Peel. Whiz in the food processor.

Eggs with bananas and cumin

Another meal on a pita.

1 teaspoon of butter or oil
2 ripe bananas, peeled and chopped coarsely
½ Spanish onion, peeled and chopped finely
1 teaspoon of ground cumin
3 eggs, beaten
salt and pepper to taste

Melt butter in a frypan and add the chopped onion. When it is soft, add the chunks of banana and the ground cumin, salt and pepper. Let the banana brown on two sides.

Add the beaten eggs and stir gently until set, about a minute. Serve on warm pita, with a little salad on the side, for a delicious supper.

Interesting Casseroles

1. Moussaka

I have produced this dish for my family many times, and for groups as large as 100 hungry film technicians. It has been declared delicious, even by those who didn't think they liked eggplant. This recipe serves 6 to 8 and is even better the next day.

3 eggplants
olive oil
1 chopped onion
3 cloves of chopped garlic
4 roma tomatoes, chopped
one handful of chopped parsley
2 cups of tomato sauce
1 bay leaf,
oregano, salt and pepper to taste
1 teaspoon of ground cinnamon
béchamel sauce (recipe on the next page)

Bechamel: ½ cup of grated parmesan
2 cups of milk
1 tablespoon of butter
3 eggs
¼ cup of flour

Slice the eggplant crosswise ⅓ inch thick. Lay the slices in a colander and sprinkle with coarse salt. Leave to sweat for a half hour. Rinse the slices and roll them tightly in a teatowel to squeeze out moisture.

Brush the slices with olive oil on both sides and broil them until brown, not black, on both sides. Lay them, overlapping, in a greased oven-proof 9 x 13 pan. Lay half the slices first.

Meanwhile, make the sauce. Fry the chopped onion in a couple of tablespoons of olive oil until wilted. Add the garlic, the tomatoes, bay leaf, a good pinch of oregano, salt and pepper and stir until tomatoes are starting to droop. Add the tomato sauce and cinnamon and bring to a simmer.

Reduce heat, cover and cook gently for 20 minutes. Check the seasoning.

Dump this sauce over the slices of broiled eggplant in the 9 x 13 pan, and cover it with the remaining eggplant slices, overlapping them to fit the pan.

For the béchamel sauce:

Put 1½ cups of milk in a little bowl with the butter and nuke it in your microwave until the butter is melted.

In a saucepan, put the ½ cup of milk and the ¼ cup of flour and whisk while heating. Add the three eggs, beating continuously. When smooth, pour in the hot milk/butter, stirring and keep stirring over medium heat until it starts to thicken, maybe 3 minutes.

Pour this over the eggplant and sprinkle the cheese over the top.

Bake 30 minutes at 350° F, and then raise the heat to 400°F for the last 15 minutes. The top will brown beautifully. Bring the moussaka out to sit for 15 more minutes before serving.

2. My Bharta

I'm very proud of this bharta—it's got loads of flavour, and it's not complicated to make. As I was picking up takeout food from our favourite Indian restaurant one time, I delivered to them a plateful of this. Later I phoned for the review. I passed. They said it was "good, surprisingly good." I guess the surprise was because I'm, you know, a shiksa.

1 large glossy eggplant
½ Spanish onion, finely chopped
1 inch cube of peeled, grated ginger
2 cloves of minced garlic
2 teaspoons each of coriander seed, cumin seed, ground
1 teaspoon each of turmeric, garam masala
½ teaspoon each of salt, pepper, dried red chili flakes
1 teaspoon fish sauce
1 teaspoon tamarind or tamarind chutney* (optional)
   (See next page to learn about tamarind.)
1 cup of frozen peas
2 chopped roma tomatoes
1 tin of coconut milk

Peel the eggplant, cube it, and salt it, let it sit in a colander to sweat for a half hour, then rinse it and squeeze it dry in a teatowel.

In a broad saucepan or stove-proof casserole pot, heat 2 tablespoons of vegetable oil and add the onion, garlic and ginger. Stir until the onion is wilted.

Add the eggplant and cook over medium low heat, stirring, until the eggplant cubes begin to colour, maybe ten minutes.

Add the other ingredients, cover and simmer gently until the eggplant is really squishy, about a half hour. Mash it down with a potato masher for a sloppy effect, and check for seasoning. You might like to add a tiny bit of brown sugar.

About the tamarind: it's sold in a rather dry block, about the consistency of dried figs. You cut off a bit and soak it in boiled water for a half hour, then strain the liquid into your cooking. Or, buy the tamarind chutney; there are several varieties available in East Indian grocery stores. It's a delicious condiment, good for lots of different uses, such as with avocado on a slice of toast, or beside any basmati rice incarnation.

3. Spicy Chicken (or Red Snapper)

Think palm trees. This is a great and generally acclaimed recipe which I've produced regularly for 30 years.

1 whole chicken cut into four pieces (or more) or
1 pound of red snapper filets, cut into 2" cubes
½ cup of flour
½ teaspoon each of salt, pepper and paprika
2 tablespoons of coconut oil or vegetable oil
1 tin of whole roma tomatoes with the juice*
1 cup of prunes
½ cup of stuffed olives
2 firm bananas
½ teaspoon of dried red chili flakes or to taste
½ teaspoon of thyme
2 bay leaves
3 cloves of garlic, minced
½ Spanish onion
6 or 7 slim carrots, chopped in 1" lengths
salt and pepper

Put the flour in a brown paper bag and add the salt, pepper and paprika. Put the chicken pieces or fish chunks in the bag, one at a time, and shake. Remove the chicken. Heat the oil in a broad frypan or stove-proof casserole pot with a lid. Brown the chicken pieces or fish in this pan on both sides. Remove and set aside. Chicken is more forgiving than fish—you can brown it without getting too agitated. The fish should only be on the oil for a half minute, or one minute

103

tops, per side. This is because while it is sitting there "aside," it's still quietly cooking, and fish doesn't need much of that.

Dump out most of the fat and add the onion and carrots to the pan. Cook, stirring, until the onions wilt. Add the garlic, the tomatoes and their juice, the bay leaves, thyme, and chili flakes. Poke at the tomatoes to break them up a bit, and bring to the boil.

Put the chicken, not the fish, back into the pot, add the prunes, cover, and cook over medium low heat for about twenty minutes, until carrots are tender. Now add the olives and bite-sized chunks of banana. Stir, cover again and cook 3 or 4 minutes more. If using fish, add it just before serving, allowing 2 minutes or so for it to warm through.

Serve with polenta, or rice, or mashed potatoes.

*If you prefer to use fresh tomatoes, use 4 or 5 chopped roma tomatoes, and a half cup of chicken stock to make up the liquid.

4. Vegetable Couscous

1 small butternut squash, peeled, seeded, and chopped in large
    chunks
4 shiny zucchini, chopped crosswise in 1" chunks
1 Spanish onion, chopped finely
4 cloves of garlic chopped
1 big tin of roma tomatoes with the juice
⅔ cup of dry chick peas or a tin, rinsed and drained
2 bay leaves
a pinch of saffron
salt and pepper
1 tablespoon of ground cumin
½ teaspoon of cinnamon
1½ cups of dry couscous
1½ cups of vegetable stock *
1 cup of chopped, toasted almonds

If using dry chick peas, rinse them and put them in a pot with water to cover and bring them to the boil. Reduce heat and cover the pot, and let them cook for about 45 minutes, checking now and then and adding water to cover if needed.

Put the chunks of squash, bay leaves and the vegetable stock into a large pot and bring to a boil. Turn down the heat, cover, and let simmer until the squash is tender-crisp, about ten minutes. Dump this out into a sieve suspended over a bowl and SAVE the cooking water.

Into this bowl with the cooking water, add the dry couscous. Stir and let sit until the liquid is absorbed. Fluff it up from time to time with a fork.

Return the pot to heat and add 2 tablespoons of vegetable oil. Fry the onion and garlic until limp. Add the tomatoes with their juice, saffron, cumin and cinnamon, zucchini chunks, and cooked chick peas, with any cooking water that remains with them. Don't add the liquid from tinned chick peas—it's yucky. When this has simmered for 3 or 4 minutes, add the cooked squash and stir gently. Check for seasoning and add salt and pepper freely.

On a warm platter, mound the hot couscous. Make a well in the centre and dump on the vegetables and whatever juice is in the pan. Sprinkle the almonds on top and serve happily. Pita is nice on the side, as well as the ubiquitous harissa, and a dish of yogourt.

CHAPTER SEVEN

puberty

Now the fit hits the shan. Your kids are growing like crazy, they feel crazy most of the time, they want instant food and they also want designer food. They have fashion madness. They're obsessed with their looks, they're worried about their pimples. Girls want to stay slim, boys want to be big and strong. They want more food, period. In their minds, chips and gravy are okay for lunch because it's fast and filling, but what they need is more protein, more iron and calcium, more carbohydrates, and more often than ever before or again in their lives.

And they want to make their own stuff, since they want independence in every possible avenue.

So our job clearly is to stock the fridge with the stuff they'll find and consume, and to cook quick, clean food, that they can copy. Ah-ha!

This means salads, quick ingredients washed and ready, covered containers of raw trimmed vegetables left handy in the fridge, bowls of fresh fruit on the table, dried fruits somewhere reliably in the cupboard, breads, cheeses. Soups, pasta, omelettes and interesting condiments are regular stomach stuffers. Leftover heaven.

They keep growing, that's the thing. Further, there are so many interesting foods to captivate their attention, fill their lunchboxes and nourish their adorable bodies.

With cooking, kids can impress their friends, that's one part: there's always something (else) they can do on a date. But the really big thing is that years of cooking together is a nice bond for families. Who among us has not at least one recipe of Gramma's or Mom's that we love to reproduce from time to time? When families cook together, everyone has a hand in preparing the food, there's some gossip and some mayhem, and everyone eats. The kids end up with a feel for the process, an interest, and a dinner. It's pretty perfect.

What we are developing here, in the land of gorgeous Emeril, sweet Fat Ladies, saucy Tamales, is a reference book kids pull off the shelf for the Way We Like It. This is a book about families. You love your children, you tend them, you hug them, you hope for them. When their tricycles are slow you wait up for them, when they're late back from the movies you wait up for them again. You scold and rage and make mistakes, and then you make amends and remember why you love them. And sometimes the family sits down to eat, and it isn't too bad.

Our eldest kids are twenty and so far they've cooked up some pretty fantastic meals for their father and me, starting with the boiled eggs they served us in bed for our fifth wedding anniversary breakfast. The toast and tea had been ready for about two hours, but the intact egg shells were delicately sprinkled with salt and pepper, just the way we like them. And the girls got in the bed with us to watch us eat.

And now they'll pass an hour making a nice sushi maki for a snack and ask if we'd like some? Meanwhile, their seven-year younger brother is deftly flipping bacon for his lunch, bravely wearing an oven mitt to thwart splatters, and their middle sibling is measuring ingredients for a pound cake she'll produce if everyone will kindly get out of her way. I do feel some satisfaction that they know their way around a kitchen: it's not a bad place to hang out.

Fridge Stocking

What's important is what is there, when they open the fridge, their bodies screaming for food.

They want something fast, but fast food isn't good food. So you stock the fridge with great stuff that they can make almost fast, and impress their friends, and satisfy their bellies, and get on with everything else that is more interesting.

One quick answer is: condiments. You have a couple of kinds of bread on hand, three kinds of cheese, tomatoes, maybe an avocado or a mango, and yike! the coriander chutney! It just makes the meal!

The other quick answer is, in this age of microwavery, leftovers. Noodly things, or vegetable salady things, or spicy things, even JUST NOODLES THAT ARE ALREADY BOILED. Amazing, but little tortelini or fusilli can be enormously tempting if they are sitting there ready for nuking, happy Parmesan already on them, a bit of attractive leftover chicken, green beans, whatever it was that you ate yesterday, or just good old spaghetti, THEY'LL EAT IT.

"Mom? Are there any more roasted peppers?"

You can't believe your ears, and it's happening to you.

From time to time you get time to make stuff together. We do at my house, but I know not everyone is as kitchen-focussed as I am.

We actually think making Vietnamese spring rolls is a fun family project. Ho hum. Other families probably bikeride or catch muskelunge.

Some weekends you might like to cook together and make Thai or Vietnamese goodies, or tempura, or a nice Indian feast. This is cooking as recreation, as family time together, and as great food.

In this Chapter

There are themes which develop, such as the Asian section, which is here to hint at some of the great things you can make that are basically Asian, including spring rolls, both deep fried and fresh, and the sauces that accompany them; Spicy Shrimp and Eggplant, Cantonese Noodles and Yummy Stir Fries. There's a design here. It leads to the starch section, including rices, risotto, phyllo and polenta. That's followed by pasta in its amazing variety. And is logically followed by pizza.

The idea is to suggest the reach for self-expression, in the fridge and on the range. At the end, we have the recipes for an eating together section including cheese fondue, bagna cauda, and "Chinese Fondue", all great ways to share a pot. Also some recipes for pots of mussels.

A Small Asian Food Section

Pad Thai

At first glance, the blend of sauce ingredients seems incompatible, but hey, if you're stuck for time, this works, and kids love it.

For the sauce:
⅓ cup of ketchup
⅓ cup of peanut butter
⅓ cup of soya sauce
1 tablespoon of fish sauce
juice of a half lime
1 teaspoon of worchestershire sauce
3 or 4 drops of sesame oil
1 tablespoon of President's Choice Memories of Thailand (optional)
1 teaspoon of sugar
water to thin to desired consistency

For the noodles:
1 package rice vermicelli
Pour boiling water over the noodles and let stand in a large bowl for 3-5 minutes, or until softened. Drain well and reserve noodles in a bowl of cold water.
In the large frypan or wok, fry in a little oil:
1 tablespoon of minced garlic
1 tablespoon of minced ginger
2 breasts of chicken, skinned, boned, sliced in thin strips
2 cups of drained cubed tofu
Stir fry this until chicken is no longer pink. Make a well in the centre of the chicken/tofu and add:
2 beaten eggs
Stir until eggs are set.

Now drain the rice noodles well, and add half of them to the stir fry pan. Add half the sauce and stir well. Mix in the rest of the noodles and sauce and serve.

Spicy Eggplant with Shrimp
(serves 4)

2 tablespoons of corn or peanut oil
1 pound of shrimp
4 Japanese eggplants
½ Spanish onion
3 green onions
1 large green pepper
10 fresh water chestnuts (optional)
1 tablespoon of chopped garlic
2 inches of peeled fresh ginger sliced thinly in rounds
3 tablespoons of soya sauce and 1 tablespoon of brown sugar
     OR 3 tablespoons of hoi sin sauce
½ teaspoon of red chili flakes (or to taste)
2 tablespoons of cornstarch dissolved in 1 cup water

   Peel the raw shrimp and set aside. Chop the long eggplant crosswise into 1-inch chunks. Chop the Spanish onion coarsely, and green onions into 1-inch lengths. Seed the green pepper and chop it coarsely. Peel the water chestnuts if you are using them, rinse and cut them in half. Peel and slice the ginger and chop the garlic. Add the soya sauce and sugar, or the hoi sin sauce to the water and cornstarch.

   In a hot wok or a large hot frypan, add the oil, the eggplant, the Spanish onion and the green pepper. Stir to coat with oil and fry for about 3 minutes, letting the vegetables brown slightly. Add the ginger, the garlic, green onion and the shrimp and stir fry until the shrimp are uniformly pink, about 2 minutes. Keep everything moving.

   Lower the heat to medium and add everything else. Bring back to the boil and stir until the cornstarch thickens and the sauce looks silky. Serve with plain steamed rice, or crispy noodles (see Cantonese Chicken Noodle, page 114).

   Variation: Also good served on top of a head of iceberg lettuce that you have cut into about eight wedges, washed, drained and arranged on a serving platter. The hot stir-fry cooks the lettuce just a bit, leaving some parts crunchy, some smooth.

Yummy Stir-Fry

There are fifty ways to go, or a hundred. Any leftover vegetable is lovely seared briefly in a frypan or wok with leftover rice, and an egg plopped on top and stirred till set, or instead, a blob of tofu. Anoint with soya sauce—that's dinner and most of the food groups.

Slightly fancier:
1 pound of firm tofu drained, or 2 boneless chicken breasts, cut in strips
1-inch square piece of fresh ginger, peeled and grated
2 cloves of garlic, finely chopped
1 tablespoon of peanut oil or vegetable oil
2 tablespoons of hoi sin sauce (molasses is an excellent alternative)
1 cup of trimmed snow peas or broccoli, cut thinly
2 teaspoons of cornstarch dissolved in
1 cup of water or stock

Optionally:
10 water chestnuts*, peeled and sliced
1 teaspoon of sesame oil
¼ cup of coriander leaves, chopped
2 green onions, trimmed and sliced lengthwise
2 tablespoons each of sesame seeds and sunflower seeds

LaSoyarie makes a great firm organic tofu square. Cut it into ¾ inch cubes, roll them in sunflower seed oil and set on a cookie sheet that is lined with parchment paper or foil. Bake at 400°F for about 20 minutes, or until crispy.

If using them, put sesame and sunflower seeds in a dry wok or frypan and place over high heat for about a minute, just to toast them briefly. Set them aside.

Add peanut oil to the same hot pan, and then the ginger and garlic, and stir. If using chicken breasts, add the strips now and cook, stirring, until most of the pink chicken colour has turned white. Add broccoli or snow peas, and let cook about 3 minutes, stirring and frying.

If using the tofu, add it to the pan now, and combine the ingredients.

In a cup, combine hoi sin sauce or molasses, sesame oil, corn starch and water, and stir to dissolve. Pour this over the vegetables. Add sliced water chestnuts, and cook, stirring, as it thickens, about 2 more minutes. Pour the whole mess out onto the platter, or in combination with some wonderful starch du jour.

Garnish with coriander and green onion spears. Serves 2 or 3.

*Fresh water chestnuts are just light-years better than tinned, but they are fussier, and not everyone has them at the corner store. You could substitute cashews, or omit, or whatever. We are not obliged to suffer.

Thai Chicken and Basil

John LeCarré was reported to have said after the opening of the film *Russia House*, based on his novel, that if the novel were a cow, the movie was a bouillion cube. I'm afraid I have done a similar disservice to this recipe as presented by Madhur Jaffery. However, like the movie, the result is awfully good; unlike the movie, you can make it in about 8 minutes.

5 cloves of garlic
3 green onions, chopped
1 inch cube of fresh ginger, peeled and grated
1 teaspoon of dried red chili flakes or to taste
1 tablespoon of dried basil or ¼ cup of fresh basil, chopped
1 pound of ground chicken
2 tablespoons of fish sauce
1 teaspoon of brown sugar
juice from one lime

Brown the chicken in sunflower seed or another vegetable oil, over medium-high heat, breaking it up as it cooks. When it is no longer pink, make a space for the seasonings and toss in the garlic, ginger, basil, and chili flakes. Stir vigorously and when you sense that the chicken is done (no pink, some nice brown bits, and small lumps), then add the fish sauce, sugar and lime juice. Toss around to blend, pour out onto a gaudy platter and garnish with the green onion.

Wonderful served with sticky rice (recipe on page 118).

Cantonese Chicken Noodle

When I was a child we made this with top sirloin steak, which is just as delicious for those who like red meat. Serves four.

1 1-pound package of fresh cantonese style egg noodles
2-4 tablespoons of peanut oil or sunflower seed oil
4 boneless chicken breasts, sliced in strips
10 fresh water chestnuts, peeled and sliced
½ pound of fresh snow peas, trimmed or 1 cup of frozen peas
1 pound of mushrooms, sliced
2 tablespoons of cornstarch, dissolved in 2 cups of chicken stock
2 tablespoons of blackstrap molasses (or hoi sin sauce)
1 tablespoon of light soya sauce (Kikkoman is our favourite)
3 green onions (sliced lengthwise)

Place the noodles in a large bowl and cover with boiling water for 1 minute. Drain.

Oil a large hot frypan, and arrange a quarter of the noodles evenly over the surface of the pan to fry. When the noodles start to brown, flip them over like a pancake, adding a little more oil, and fry on the other side until it is also lightly brown. Put this nest of noodles on a large serving platter or baking dish in a warm oven to hold it. Fry another batch of noodles the same way until all the noodles are done.

Put the last of the oil in the same hot frypan and add the strips of chicken breast. Flip them around until there is no pink visible, lower the heat to medium, cover and cook until the strips are just firm, maybe three minutes. Using a slotted spoon, place the strips on top of the warm crispy noodles, keeping as much fat in the pan as you can. Now add the mushrooms to the pan, raise the heat and fry for 2 minutes, or until they start to brown. Then stir them.

Add the snow peas (or frozen peas) and the water chestnuts and stir fry until the snow peas are beginning to soften, or the frozen peas are no longer frozen.

Dissolve the cornstarch in a little cool water and add it, with the molasses and the Kikkoman, to the chicken stock. Stir and dump it onto the mushrooms and peas. (If you are using beef, use beef stock.) Stir this around until the sauce is thickened and bubbling, a minute or two. Now take the platter of noodles and chicken out of the oven and pour the vegetables over top. Garnish with the green onion slivers strewn artistically, and serve. You can add chilies if you like them, more soya sauce if you want it saltier, whatever.

Vietnamese Spring Rolls (Fresh)

These rolls are refreshing and full of bright flavours. They can wait, covered and refrigerated, for 3 or 4 hours.

16 10-inch circular rice paper wrappers
16 cooked shrimp, halved lengthwise
8 small leaves of leaf lettuce
1 cup of julienned English cucumber
3 green onions, trimmed and sliced lengthwise
1 cup of fresh bean sprouts
½ cup each of fresh mint, fresh coriander, and fresh basil, sliced finely
peanut dipping sauce (recipe follows)

Submerge the rice papers one by one in a bowl of water and lay them out on damp tea towels side by side. Let them rest and limber up for about 5 minutes. You don't have to have them all ready at once, obviously, not many people have room in their kitchens to lay out 16 papers simultaneously. Make in batches. Lay all your ingredients out in separate little piles or in bowls around your assembly area.

Place the halves of shrimp on the bottom third of the rice paper circle. Put on top of them a few spears of julienned cucumber, of the green onion (bend or cut the onion into a two inch length), the bean sprouts, and a sprinkling of each of the herbs.

Cover this little salad with the bottom of the rice paper, fold over the left and right sides of the paper to cover, and roll the bundle up into a fairly firm little package. The paper will stick to itself to seal.

Lay the finished spring roll on a piece of lettuce, and roll up the other rice paper rolls. Serve with the peanut dipping sauce, each roll wrapped in its lettuce leaf. (Peanut dipping sauce is on next page.)

Peanut Dipping Sauce
¼ cup of peanut butter
juice of 1 lime
2 tablespoons of fish sauce
1 tablespoon each of fresh grated ginger and garlic
1 teaspoon of red chili flakes (or to taste)
Put all this in your food processor and buzz. Add enough water to make a smooth paste, maybe 2 tablespoons. Fresh lemon grass, using the lower half and chopping it very finely, is a nice addition if you can get it.

Vietnamese Spring Rolls (Fried)

This is an extremely satisfying hors d'oeuvre to make because it tastes exactly like it came from a good Thai restaurant. It's fun to make in batches, with a few participants to speed things along, or with whom to sing harmony.

¼ pound of ground pork or chicken
1 small tin of crabmeat
1 green onion, chopped finely
5 fresh water chestnuts,* peeled and chopped finely
2 tablespoons of dried black fungus*
8 dried shiitake mushrooms*
a handful of rice vermicelli (dry)
1 egg
½ teaspoon of dried red chili flakes
dash of salt and pepper
round rice papers
2 tablespoons of flour mixed with a little water to make a paste

You also need:
a bunch of fresh mint
a head of Boston lettuce or another soft lettuce
and lime sauce (recipe follows)

Soak the black fungus in boiled (still hot) water for ½ hour. This is a lovely little mushroom with a great texture and a light flavour.

They are often sandy or lumpy, so once they're limber, just feel them, and pull off and discard anything tough. Chop up the good stuff and put it in a bowl. This water is great flavouring for stirfries or sauces, though you need to strain it.

At the same time, soak the Chinese mushrooms in boiled water. Then strain and save the water if you want to. Trim off and discard the tough mushroom stems and chop up the caps, then add to the fungus.

Soak the noodles in tap water for the same half hour. When soft, chop them coarsely.

Add the ground pork and the crabmeat to the bowl with the two kinds of mushrooms. Add the chopped noodles, the green onion, the chopped water chestnut, the egg, the chilies, pepper and salt.

Soak the rice papers individually in a bowl of water, each one for about a quarter minute, and let them lie on a wet tea towel for 5 minutes or so. Do several at once, laying them out side by side.

When they feel very pliable, put a spoonful of filling on the circle, near the 6 o'clock position, but partway up toward the centre of the paper. Fold over the bottom of the rice paper, then one side, left or right, whichever, and roll the little package up toward the top, so that you have a fairly firm bundle like a little cabbage roll, that measures maybe two and a half inches long and an inch thick. Seal top edge of the envelope with the flour paste applied to the open flap, and put aside. Make another one the same way, and so on, until you don't want to make any more, or run out of filling, whichever comes first.

Now you deep fry the little fellas, in hot oil, until golden brown, drain, lay them on top of the lettuce with the mint sprigs to serve with the lime sauce.

Lime Sauce (serves 4)
1 clove of garlic, peeled and crushed
¼ cup of fish sauce (available in Chinese food stores)
¼ cup of fresh lime juice
2 tablespoons of sugar
¼ teaspoon of hot red chili flakes (or to taste)

Combine ingredients and serve in individual bowls for dipping.
Now, take your warm spring roll, wrap it in a leaf of lettuce with a sprig of mint in a package. Dip into delicious sauce. Gorgeous.

A Starch Section

Sticky Rice

Take two cups of glutinous rice, short grain, Chinese or Japanese, and rinse it in several changes of fresh water until you're tired of doing so, or sooner. Suspend the rice in a sieve over a bowl for an hour or two to let it dry.

Bring to a boil 2¼ cups of water with a tiny bit of salt. Add the rice, and immediately turn the heat to low. Cover and let it do what it does for 20 minutes. Then remove from heat, let sit undisturbed, still covered, and serve it after 20 minutes more. This rice is STICKY, and enormously fun to eat with your fingers. Think: banana leaves, coconuts. This serves four.

Brown Rice

Heat a saucepan with a little butter or oil in the bottom. Pour in a cup of brown rice and stir it around until you smell the nice nutty fragrance of rice, a minute or so. Add two cups of water, a pinch of salt, and cover the pan. When the water boils, turn the heat to low, and cook undisturbed for about 40 minutes, or until the water is absorbed and the rice is tender. Serves 4.

Additions are great. Wheat berries, sesame seeds, other rices, lentils: anything small, really. Take out a tablespoon of rice, add a tablespoon of lentils. Cook 'em with the rice from the start. Otherwise, add nuts, or whatever dried fruits you feel are appropriate, when the rice is done.

Baked Basmati Rice

Bring 3 cups of water to the boil in an oven-proof casserole dish that is equipped with a tight lid. Add 2 cups of basmati rice and 1 teaspoon of salt. When the water comes back to the boil, cover and place the casserole in a slow oven, 325°F, for about 40 minutes. This produces a very nice rice, separate, not sticky, and you don't have to watch it or fuss with it at all. You can double or triple the recipe, but you have to fudge the water a bit. For instance, if you want to serve 25 people, use 10 cups of rice to about 13 ½ cups of water.

Microwaved Risotto

Oxymoronic, you say? No, man, this is liberation. This works and it's darned good. Thank you to the good folks at Uncle Ben's for figuring this one out. Here's the basic recipe, ready for embellishments.

1 cup of arborio rice
2 cups of good chicken stock
2 tablespoons of butter
¼ cup of grated parmesan cheese

In a large microwaveable bowl, melt butter for 10 seconds on HIGH. Stir into it the arborio until all the kernels are coated with butter. Then add the stock.

Microwave uncovered on HIGH for 12 minutes, stirring once or twice during the period.

Stir again, cover with a plate, and microwave on LOW for 6 minutes. At the end, stir in the cheese, and serve.

Amazing, eh? And it's good. Al dente, creamy, the works.

You can also add stuff at the end.

For example:

1. Peeled sliced lightly fried butternut squash, just tender, and a pinch of saffron, pinch of sage, ground pepper. Stir and let sit for a few minutes. Have by itself, or with salad, or with salad and poultry, depending on your entourage.

2. Pesto, thinly sliced zucchini and toasted walnuts.

3. Grilled chopped portobello mushrooms, butter-fried with garlic and onion. Substitute stilton for parmesan. Great beside beef.

4. Many coloured peppers, chopped and fried lightly in butter, with oregano and garlic. Substitute a smoked cheese for parmesan. With pork.

5. Steamed mussels, cooked fennel, splash of pernod, pinch saffron, two small chopped tomatoes.

6. Lemon peel, artichoke hearts, pitted black olives. Substitute feta cheese for parmesan. With lamb.

Polenta

Polenta is a great alternative starch that you can serve instead of mashed potatoes or noodles, with practically any toppings, such as spaghetti sauce, or stir-fried veggies (onion, portobello mushrooms, zucchini, rapini, green beans, garlic, whatever).

The important distinction is that polenta isn't the finely ground cornmeal that we use to bake cornbread. You can use this regular North American cornmeal in the recipe below and get quite a nice product very quickly.

 1 cup of regular cornmeal
 2 cups of water or chicken stock
 2 cups of milk
 2 cobs of fresh corn (or 1 cup frozen niblets)
 ½ of a white onion, chopped finely
 2 tablespoons of olive oil or butter

In a large saucepan, heat the oil over medium heat. Add the chopped onion and stir around, letting the onion get soft. If you are using fresh corn, cut the kernels off the cobs into a bowl. Frozen corn is easier, just dump 1 cup of it in.

Add the chicken stock, or water, or milk, whatever you are using, so that you are warming up 4 cups of liquid. When it boils, turn off the heat, and sprinkle in the cornmeal, while stirring with a whisk. Switch to a wooden spoon, and stir until the polenta starts to thicken, which is really fast, like half a minute. It's fluffy and delicious, and leftovers can be microwaved. But it's not polenta.

❖   ❖   ❖

Real Polenta

You have to use coarsely ground cornmeal, which is more readily available nowadays than it was even a year ago and is usually labeled Polenta. This is a traditional dish which is more work and infinitely more wonderful to eat, with a silky and creamy texture. It can be laid out on a surface to cool, then cut into squares or triangles, and barbecued or grilled on the stove, or just fried gently in a little olive oil. Served like this, it's crispy on the outside and velvet inside.

    1 cup of polenta (coarsely ground cornmeal)
    4 cups of liquid, half water, half milk, or chicken stock, or
        vegetable broth
    ½ teaspoon of salt

Bring the liquid to a boil in a big heavy-bottomed casserole pot and add the salt. Turn down the heat to medium low. While stirring constantly with a whisk, sprinkle in all the polenta grains, "like a fine rain," until you have one smooth loose potful. Turn the heat to low.

Now switch to a wooden spoon and stir thoroughly, not constantly but every couple of minutes, as the polenta thickens. If you intend to serve the polenta later, stir it for 10 or 15 minutes, since you will be cooking it more on the grill or whatever. If you want to serve it soft, stir for about 25 or 30 minutes, and serve with great satisfaction, with melting cheeses or buttery mushrooms or a rich beef stew or chicken liver chasseur or whatever the heck you feel like.

Things to Do with Phyllo

There are dozens of things to do with this paper-thin pastry. You buy it frozen in the supermarket, and when you're getting ready to use it, you let it thaw for an hour or so on the kitchen counter. When it will unroll easily, do so. It dries out fast so you need to cover the exposed sheets with a teatowel while you are working on your project.

Phyllo Pizza

¼ cup of butter (melted)
¼ cup of olive oil

Have ready a cookie sheet. Use a baster to brush the mixture of melted butter and olive oil all over the surface of the tin. Lay one sheet of phyllo to cover the cookie sheet, and brush it with the butter/oil. Lay another sheet of phyllo over the first and brush this one too. The number of layers you use relates directly to the outcome of the pizza. Four sheets is too few, ten is excessive. Butter each one until you've had enough of the whole thing.

2 ripe tomatoes (sliced thinly)
1½ cups of grated cheese (provolone is fine, or mozzarella or asiago, or combo thereof)
1 or 2 cloves of garlic, chopped finely
2 teaspoons of dried basil
1 teaspoon of ground black pepper

Distribute the slices of tomato side by side across the top layer of phyllo. Sprinkle the minced garlic, basil and pepper over the tomatoes, and the grated cheese over all. Be light-handed with your toppings, or the crust won't get crisp.

Bake in a 400°F oven until the edges of the phyllo are browned and the cheese is melted, 15 or 20 minutes.

This pizza is fine hot or at room temperature. The phyllo stays crisp and the layers are luxuriously crunchy. A good thing to take to a party.

Phyllo Pockets

Prepare your phyllo sheets as above, and then cut the rectangles into squares that are about 3 or 4 inches on each side. These you place decoratively into the cups of muffin pans, and bake until golden, maybe 5-7 minutes in a hot oven. Now you can stuff them with anything whatsoever, for hors d'oeuvres, entrée accompaniment, or dessert:

Cold
cajun shrimp, tomatillos and avocado
sundried tomato purée with a blob of pesto and a black olive
curried chicken salad with apples
hummos, strips of roasted red pepper, and chèvre
cream cheese and raspberries
a brownie square topped with whipped cream

Hot
For hot options, fill the cups BEFORE baking with:

Hors d'oeuvre:
a little chunk of brie and some cranberry sauce
garlicky fried portobello mushrooms and a chunk of gorgonzola
egg, cream, ham, and chives (tiny quiches)
spinach, ricotta and feta (mini spanikopita)
a scallop and a bit of fish mousse around it
cooked mashed eggplant with tiny lamb meatballs

To serve with your main course, fill with:
creamed spinach and leeks
mashed potatoes and garlic with melted gruyère on top
carrots cooked with ginger and a splash of orange juice
carrots cooked with butter and tarragon
leftovers from your Indian take-out dinner, like aloo gobi or saag
leftovers from your Mexican take-out dinner, like refried beans
or whatever you can imagine.

For the hot things, you can change the shape of the phyllo so that
it covers the filling, if you want to, like a little samosa. Make a neat
package by turning the four top corners of the raw pastry together in
a little swirl, or fold them down to make a little box, or design a
rocket ship. Really, please yourself.

You can also put the filling on a strip of phyllo layers, fold it up
like a flag, and have lovely phyllo triangles. Brush with butter and
bake on a cookie sheet until brown and crisp. These are good for
recess snacks and lunchboxes too.

Pasta

Fusilli, basil, tomatoes and bocconcini

Boil the noodles. Always use lots and lots of water for noodles and add salt to the water. You salt the water because of osmosis, or possibly, meiosis: I'm sure you know which.

While the noodles are in there, chop beautiful roma tomatoes into little chunks. These are nice to use because they haven't much of a sloppy seed section. Wash your bunch of basil leaves and chop them in twain. Slice the little balls of bocconcini. Don't have baby mozzarella? Cut up chunks of brie instead. Extremely delicious. Regular mozzarella is also fine. Or chèvre.

Drain the twirly noodles and festoon with the tomatoes, basil and cheese. Stir. Serve with olive oil, black pepper and freshly grated Parmesan.

Allergy Note: Wheat-free quinoa noodles are available in many shapes.

Another Note: This note is about oven-dried tomatoes.

Truly something worth considering. Before you go to school or work in the morning, you take any number of plum tomatoes, cut them in half, lay them on a non-reactive baking dish, like pyrex or enamel, cut side up, and sprinkle them with coarse salt, oregano and a few red chili flakes. Set them in the oven at 225°F, and then leave the house.

When you return, your home smells marvellous, and in the oven are dried tomatoes, with a dense sweet flavour. Add them to pasta, and grate on some good parmesan, flip with some olive oil, and you have something really good, without effort. If you'll only be gone all afternoon, you can set the oven to 250°F and have them ready in four or five hours instead.

If you want to be very fancy, combine these tomatoes with whatever other vegetables you have at hand—a chopped bulb of fennel or a bunch of rapini, sautéed with a little garlic and onion are each pretty irresistible. Or you could dump this whole lovely mess onto pizza dough instead and bake up something extremely delicious.

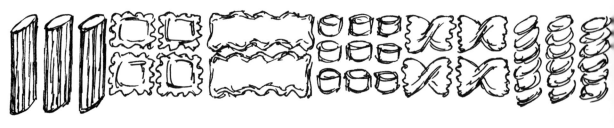

Fasta Pasta

There must be a thousand recipes that would fit in here.

Boil the cheese-stuffed tortellini, drain, add pesto. That's dinner.

◆　◆　◆

Boil the orecciette, drain, add chopped fresh pear and blobs of gorgonzola, maybe some walnuts, some julienned radiccio. Boom.

◆　◆　◆

Boil the radiatore, drain. Barbecue, broil or grill slices of fennel and heads of garlic. (Garlic may be barbecued and broiled unpeeled. Trim off and discard the top half inch from the whole head, and nestle the bulb in a little foil cup, drizzled with a bit of olive oil. When soft, 40 minutes or so, cool and peel the sweet soft garlic buds and add to anything.)

Or, fry the slices of fennel in olive oil with a clove or two of chopped garlic. When the fennel is tender, add to pasta, with blobs of creamy goat cheese, toasted sunflower seeds, ground black pepper. Sigh.

◆　◆　◆

Boil the orzo, drain. Chop zucchini or summer squash or both, rapini and garlic and fry for 4 minutes in olive oil. Toss in with the noodles, and then add chopped fresh thyme, grated parmesan reggiano, you're done.

◆　◆　◆

Boil the penne, and while it's boiling, gently fry peeled bite-sized slices of butternut squash in olive oil or butter. Add chopped sage leaves, or dry if you don't have fresh, and salt and pepper. Drain noodles when they're done, add squash, and grate good Swiss gruyère on top. Excellent.

◆　◆　◆

Boil the little shell pasta, and while that's going on, cut corn off the cob, and fry in butter with a little chopped white onion and some chopped seeded red bell pepper. Drain the pasta, add the corn and peppers, and grate a cup of smoked jarlsberg on top. Wow.

◆ ◆ ◆

Boil the capellini in plenty of water, stirring frequently, not very long. It takes about 3 or 4 minutes. Drain. Add anything. Today add yesterday's leftover Spicy Eggplant with Shrimp (see page 111). Tomorrow add leftover bharta....(page 102).

Pizza

Just get it from the dairy case of your grocery store, fine. Or make your own. Roll it out, put wonderful things on it, lay it on a cookie sheet that you sprinkled liberally with cornmeal, or on a non-stick perforated pizza pan, and bake at 450° F for 15 or 20 minutes, until the crust is golden and stiff. Piece of cake. This recipe I call the Two or Four Method, because everything is either a measure of 2 or 4, and it produces two 14" pizza crusts.

Pizza Dough

2 cups of warm water
4 teaspoons of active dry yeast
4 cups of all purpose flour
2 teaspoons of salt
¼ cup of olive oil
extra flour and olive oil

Measure the flour and salt into a large bowl. Mix warm water and yeast in a measuring cup, and let it sit for 5 minutes until frothy. Add the olive oil and stir this mixture into the flour. Leave it to think for about ten minutes. During this time, the flour rests and expands and what was formerly a sticky mess is transformed into a manageable mess.

Dump out the dough onto a floured surface to knead. Work it by hand for a good five minutes, folding the dough and gently pressing it down with the heel of your hand, folding, pressing, and adding more flour as you go. It will start off very soft and sticky, and a dough scraper is really handy here. You lift the dough off the work surface, sprinkle flour underneath, plop the dough back down, sprinkle more flour on the top, and keep kneading. Eventually you have a smooth springy ball with only a hint of stickiness. But you do want that little bit of residual stickiness as it relates directly to the crispiness of your pizza.

Oil the inside of a clean bowl and put the ball of dough into it, turning the ball so it gets oil all over. Cover the bowl and put it in a warm place to rise (proof) for an hour, until doubled in bulk. Go outside, read a book, write your master's thesis.

Punch down the risen ball, to let the air out of the mass.

Divide the ball in two. On a lightly floured surface, gently roll out the dough with a rolling pin into a shape that looks like a pizza and place it on a cookie sheet that has been oiled and sprinkled with cornmeal, or on a non-stick perforated pizza pan. Festoon the toppings *du jour*, pop in a hot oven (450°F), enjoy in about 20 minutes, when the crust edge is brown and crisp. Slide the pizza onto a rack to cool while you make another one the same way.

Possible Toppings

grilled eggplant slices covered by grated provolone
sautéed eggplant cubes, onions and garlic, slathered under provolone
ovendried tomato purée with asiago
fennel slices, goat cheese, and garlic (a personal favourite)
broccoli, red onion, black olive, chunks of brie cheese
sliced tomatoes, pesto blobs, parmesano reggiano
creamed spinach, feta cheese, tomato and oregano

And so on, endlessly delicious.

Chinese Fondue

Sometimes you find this wonderful buffet style meal in Chinese restaurants. It's really a treat. To prepare it at home is a snap.

You need about 3 cups of good chicken stock or tom yam broth (see page 56) in a broad mouthed (earthenware) pot that you have on the table over a warmer. The interesting part is the variety you can provide of dip-ables. You need:

tofu cubes
mushrooms of many varieties, wild and tame
seafoods like peeled shrimps, scallops, crab claws, chunks of fish (haddock, snapper, salmon)
chicken skinned and boned and cut into chunks
beef, cubed, if you are into it
vegetables like bok choy, mustard greens, snow peas, nappa cabbage, broccoli, sprouts, all that kind of thing

Each person cooks a selected thing in the common stock pot for however long they feel they would like to. Condiments are the thing:

hot mustard, hoi sin sauce, plum sauce, black bean sauce,
chili oil, sesame oil and all sorts of delicious things that you can
buy in Oriental food stores

At the end you divide up the remaining (by now incredible) broth into individual bowls, and plonk in rice noodles that have been soaked for an hour or two in water until soft, with some fresh coriander leaves. Fantastic.

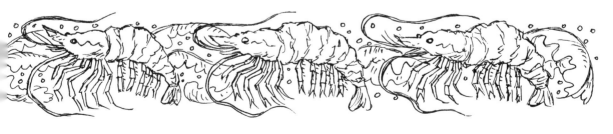

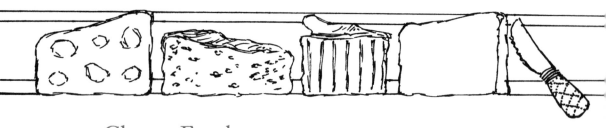

Cheese Fondue

I told you about my dear, other, Swiss mom. This is her recipe. For 4 to 6 people:

2 cups of dry white wine (*"un petit verre pour chacun"*)
3 cloves of garlic, peeled, halved

You poach the garlic in the wine in a solid glazed earthenware pot. A large heavy-bottomed saucepan is okay if that's what you have. We are not even talking "simmer" here, we are looking at little bubbles forming on the sides of the pot, which is over low heat. This could take 10 or 15 minutes.

Grate:
1 pound of real Swiss gruyère and no substitute will do
½ pound of edam
½ pound of mozzarella

Mix the grated cheeses together in a bowl. When the wine is steaming, remove the garlic, raise the heat to medium and begin adding the cheese while stirring all the time with a wooden spoon. You have to stay with this. Turn on the oven to 200°F and pop in a loaf Italian bread to crisp up.

Gradually you add all the cheese, putting in more as the mess melts. Now you have a slurry of cheese with perhaps a liquid surface. You solve this problem by mixing 1 tablespoon of cornstarch with 3 tablespoons of kirsch, or optionally, more white wine. Kirsch is, of course, the traditional way to go, but I don't hold on it for flavour. Also, there's a Swiss thing of adding about a quarter cup of heavy cream, which seems superfluous, but it's up to you.

Dump in the cornstarch mixture and stir gently. The cheese will bind up with any residual liquid and be one smooth beautiful mass. Turn off the heat. Take the bread out of the oven and cut it into 1-inch slices that you then cut into bite-sized squares. Place them in a bread basket, put the fondue in the centre of your dining table over a warming candle or on a hot plate and dip freely. You need low steady heat: fondue does not take to rewarming. At the end, the crust on the bottom of the pot is the best part.

The long forks are useful; they protect you from the stringy delicious HOT cheese that you roll onto your bread. Think warm alpine châteaux. Good red wine, a soft lettuce salad with dijon dressing, maybe some cornichons or pickled pearl onions. This is what we like to have on Christmas Eve.

Bagna Cauda

You can dunk any vegetables in this warm fondue-style appetizer dip, but rapini and fennel are way better than any others. Young cardoons are traditional, which means that in their absence, lightly steamed artichokes will do. Asparagus is also very nice, or broccoli if you can't get rapini. Zucchini is good. Really, though, you can have it with nothing else but rapini and be perfectly happy.

For 6 to 8 persons, in your little earthenware (or, all right, metal) fondue pot you put:
¾ cup of olive oil
3 tablespoons of butter
2 teaspoons of finely chopped garlic
1 tiny tin of flat anchovy fillets, chopped (the filets, not the tin)
1 teaspoon of salt

Place your warmer in the middle of the table. I find that a section of newspaper is not too ugly underneath the warmer, and it saves the table from this very drippy antipasto.

On the stove, heat the olive oil and the butter until the butter just begins to foam. Add the garlic and anchovies and cook over VERY low heat until the anchovies dissolve into a paste. Stir frequently. When you have achieved anchovy paste-dom, add the salt and place the pot on your warming candle on the table.

Meanwhile, wash the vegetables and trim off obvious tough stems or blemishes. You can have a large tray of the veggies that everyone chooses, or you can prepare individual plates in an arranged style. Each person dips the vegetables, swirling a bit to keep the oil and sediment mixed. Good crusty Italian bread is essential, and a fine minestrone soup afterward, and some simple pasta, makes a great meal.

Some Things to Do with Mussels

Mussels are good for us, and they are extremely flexible in presentation. The standard has gotta be this:

1 pound of mussels, cleaned
1 shallot diced
½ cup of dry white wine
2 tablespoon of butter
1 loaf French baguette

Doesn't that look familiar already? Classic French approach. Scrub your mussels, which you don't even have to do if they are cultured ones. Discard any mussels which have broken shells, and any that don't close when you inspect them.

In a large pot, melt the butter and gently wilt the shallot. Add the wine and let reduce over medium heat for a few minutes. Don't wait until the pan is dry, and then add the mussel shells. Cover, and simmer until the shells open, maybe 5 minutes. Stir things around if you like, it won't hurt. Discard any mussels that don't open.

You want open shells, but you want mussels inside which are still plump. (Over-done looks like this tiny little wizened dot inside the shell, don't do that to your mussels.) Dump all this out into a festive bowl and let everyone dunk in their bread and grab their share.

Mussels Thai style

1 tin of coconut milk
a few chilies, maybe 3 dried red chilies
3 lime leaves
2 stalks of lemon grass, coarsely chopped.

Combine these ingredients in a large pot, and then reduce the coconut milk by half, and add the mussels. Steam as you did above. Serve with a baguette to sop up juices.

Or you can go Italian, with tomatoes, fennel and basil.

Or Indian style, Goan-style mussels are famous
2 pounds of mussels
1" cube ginger and 8 cloves garlic blenderized together
1 chopped onion
¼ cup of oil
1 teaspoon of dried red chili flakes
½ teaspoon of turmeric
2 teaspoons of ground cumin
½ cup of coconut milk
½ teaspoon of salt

 Heat oil in a large saucepan and wilt the onion. Add the ginger/garlic purée, and all other ingredients, not the mussels. Add a cup of water and let simmer until reduced by half. Add the mussels, stir, cover and let steam until the mussels open. Serve with great Indian bread (puri, naan, etc) and basmati.

Rewarding Bread Baking

The misconception about bread is that you make it all at once, like pie. Say you see some of the lovely peaches in your six-quart basket are getting a bit past it and you say, "I'll make pie with those." That is a completely acceptable and reasonable strategy. You can whip up the pie on the spot. Bread is not like this.

It seems that the more other things you have to do besides make bread, the better. Bread is a step-by-step thing, requiring very little work for each step, but long stretches of time between them. During these times the yeast develops, or the gluten rests, or the flavours merge, or the carbon dioxide is produced. It's a wonderland of activity that you don't have to lay one finger to most of the time.

It was Laurie Colwin who opened my eyes to this fact, in her wonderful book *Home Cooking*. She relates the saga of her release from enslavement to bread, and provides a recipe so enchanting I made no other bread than that one, week after week, for about six months. But then I discovered sponge starter.

Sponge starter brings to bread an extra day of preparation. It also gives breads depth of flavour and vitality that straight yeast breads can't match. Sponge starter is sort of a sourdough shortcut. This is how you make one.

Sponge Starter (Day One of Bread)

Before you go to school on, say, a Thursday morning, you take:

¾ cup of warm filtered water (110°F: feels very warm, not blazing)
1½ cups of all-purpose unbleached flour
⅛ teaspoon of active dry yeast
and you mix these together in a plastic or glass container. I use a plastic container that used to have 2 kilograms of peanut butter in it. It has a lid and straight sides, and that's what is needed here. A big clean glass mason jar would be fine too.

Place the lid loosely on the jar and shake the contents vigorously.

The mixture will be very stiff and gummy. Place the lid on the jar but don't screw it on: air should come in and out. Put the jar somewhere warm: I place mine on my telephone answering machine, which works fine, although if you have a gas stove, there's a warm spot in the centre of the range, over the pilot light. Leave it there all day. I know there are a lot of things to think about before school, but this actually only takes five minutes. You can do it while your waffle is toasting.

When you come home, your sponge will have risen to at least three times its former self. Put it in the fridge overnight. You have to use it within three days, perhaps using one of the recipes below.

Day Two Friday after school you combine the ingredients below, knead the dough, and then let it rise for an hour before you put it in the fridge overnight.

Egg and Yogourt Bread

You need three bread pans for this project. Medium-sized grocery store foil pans are fine. Your hands will be covered with goop so take off your rings.

Beat together:
¾ cup of plain yogourt
2 eggs in a bowl and then set aside for a minute.
In another bowl combine:
1 cup of bran
1 cup of wheat germ
½ cup of flax seed (optional)
1 cup of rolled oats that you have buzzed in the blender to make floury
1 tablespoon of salt
Stir this together and set aside.

Combine in a very big ceramic or glass bowl (hereafter called the bread bowl):
3 cups of warm filtered water
1 teaspoon of active dry yeast

all your sponge starter (recipe above)

Mix together and work with your fingers until the sponge is really loose. Add the egg/yogourt mixture and stir again, and then dump in the bran and oat mixture. Now! You will need:

6 to 8 cups all purpose unbleached flour which you add to the wet stuff, stirring, a few cups at a time. For instance, add 5 cups into the bread bowl, stir it up as well as you can with the wooden spoon, and then when it becomes too difficult, turn ALL the dough out onto a work surface to knead it with your hands. Keep the mass together, turning it, pressing it down, and folding it over onto itself, gradually adding as much more flour as you need to make a fairly unsticky mass.

Those steel, straight-edged, rectangular-shaped dough cutters are wonderful for this job (the word "indispensable" is trying to come out here): you use one to scrape the sticky dough up off the counter and fold it back over onto itself. Sprinkle on more flour, and keep kneading. Eventually you will have a mass of dough that is not too sticky; it's all one piece, it's roundish, and it is completely blended together and homogeneous; if it's springy, that's even better. Kneading is the longest part of the whole ordeal and will take about ten minutes.

Put a tablespoon or so of sunflower seed oil in the same old bread bowl and plonk the dough back into it, moving it around and then flipping it over, so that there is a little bit of oil all over the dough and the bowl. Cover the bowl loosely with a plastic bag or plastic wrap and let it rise for an hour in a warm place. Take a break. Before you go out for the evening, put the bowl in the fridge overnight.

Saturday or Day Three! Incredibly, so far you have invested about 20 minutes of actual work into this project. The dough has been rising, the flavours have been developing, the bread is practically making itself. That's one of the charming things about bread.

Shaping and Baking the Loaves

Day Three Take the dough out of the fridge. Now you have a huge cold mass of dough, ready for bread pans. There's enough for three 8 x 4 inch loaves: one for today, one to freeze for later in the week, and one to give with pride to a buddy. Perfect to take with you to your friend's dinner party tonight.

Dump the mass of dough out onto your lightly floured work surface. Move it around in a friendly way, and it will deflate and soon feel resiliant in your hands. Using a knife or the trusty dough cutter, divide the dough into three equal pieces.

If you want to add things to your loaves, now is the time. You can knead in raisins and cinnamon if you like, or sunflower seeds are very nice. Over time you can experiment with various nuts and dried fruits and herbs.

Work one of the thirds of dough gently, kneading it for a few minutes to distribute the nuts or fruit that you have chosen, then roll it into a log shape and place it in an oiled breadpan. Turn it over so the prettiest side is up, and so there's a little oil all over it, and repeat with another loaf the same way (or with different ingredients. Without additions is nice too).

When your three loaves are in their pans, put them in a warm spot (like on top of the fridge) and cover them loosely with the same old plastic sheet you used before. Let them rise until doubled in bulk, which might be two or three hours, depending on the temperature of the kitchen. The dough is cold from the fridge and will start to rise sluggishly.

Heat your oven for 20 minutes before you bake to 425°F. You do this to facilitate Oven Spring, a romantic phrase meaning the loaves, thrilled by the warmth of the oven, rise a little more just before they make their crust. Dust the tops of the loaves with flour, for a country effect, or sprinkle with poppy seeds, or sesame seeds, or whatever you have handy. Flax. Oregano. Butter.

Put the loaves in the oven side by side on the middle rack and close the oven door. Fill a teacup with hot water from the tap and toss this inside the hot oven, on the SIDES of the oven, not on the loaves. Close the door. In one minute, do it again. This steam helps your loaves to achieve a glorious crust. Bake for twenty minutes at this temperature, and then reduce the temperature to 350°F for ten more minutes. Take the loaves out and admire them. Dump them out of their pans onto a rack or racks to cool. Tap the little dears on their sides or bottoms to hear the infamous "hollow sound" that means "Done." Give yourself a huge pat on the back because they look so beautiful, they will taste so good, and with all that yogourt and egg and wheat germ, they are incredibly good for you. Wait until they are cool before you slice off your first delicious piece. Plain, or toasted with jam, or with cheeses. Amazing.

If you ever weary of this wonderful bread, try the recipe below. Same deal on the Sponge Starter, and same deal on it taking three days to get results.

This time, want to try dinner rolls? (Any bread recipe will also make dinner rolls.) If you have muffin tins, let this dough rise therein, but if you are muffin tinless, put football-shaped, tennis ball-sized balls of dough on cornmeal-sprinkled cookie sheets to rise freely. Slash the tops end to end with a sharp knife, and dust the buns with flour just before you pop them in the oven. So sporty.

Sunflower Seed Oatmeal Walnut Dinner Rolls

When I was a university student, I thought the best possible birthday present for a friend was a loaf of homemade bread. However, my breads were always rock hard and one inch high. I wish I'd had this recipe then. It's easy and extremely presentable, and it makes three beautiful loaves.

It also makes extremely delicious, light, close textured rolls with a fantastic thin crispy crust. If you don't use the rolls right away, reheat them for a few minutes before dinner to restore the crunch.

Grow a sponge with the recipe and modus operandi above. Then, on day two, in your food processor, buzz:

1 cup of rolled oats until floury, and in a bowl mix it with
1 cup of wheat germ
4 cups of all purpose flour or whole wheat flour, or a combo thereof
2 teaspoons of salt

In your trusty bread bowl, mix together with your fingers:

3 cups of warm filtered water
2 teaspoons of dry yeast
all your sponge recipe, until the sponge is broken up nicely

Add the flours to the bread bowl and mix vigorously with a wooden spoon. Let this mixture rise for an hour. Then dump it out onto your floured work surface and add

1½ or more cups of all purpose flour

and knead until magically smooth and elastic. Place the dough back in the oiled bread bowl, turning it around again so everything is touched by the oil, and pop it back in the fridge overnight to let the flavours develop.

Day Three, plop the cold dough out on the work surface and add:

½ cup of chopped walnuts
½ cup of sesame seeds
½ cup of sunflower seeds

and knead until blended.

Decide if you want three loaves, two loaves and some buns, all buns, etc. Divide the dough into three and take your pick. For buns, roll equal sized, egg-sized, bits in your hands, and set them in your greased container of choice to rise until doubled. You'll get about two dozen softball-sized buns. If you'd like them daintier, make three dozen, and start smaller, like golf balls. Really oil the muffin tins: nothing is more annoying than stuck buns.

Bake at 450°F, sprinkling water twice on the sides of the oven as above for the Egg/Yogourt loaf. For buns, bake 20 minutes. For loaves, bake 20 minutes at 450°F and ten more minutes at 350°F.

These buns are wonderful at a party, served with cheese or dip, or with cold cuts and sliced tomatoes and condiments so that people can make their own sandwiches. The smaller version is a good dinner roll size.

NEWS FLASH!
This recipe makes beautiful bread in one day! Skip the sponge part, Day One, and at the end of the first rise, just proceed! The second rise is fast because the dough is warm. Start to finish, 3½ to 4 hours.

CHAPTER EIGHT

BOX LUNCHES

A nd now for the real challenge. You've given your children an interest in a range of food, shown them how to cook it, and stood back as they meticulously measured baking powder. Now they're vegan, or vegetarian, or off dairy, or pursuing iron through spinach shakes. Teens today know what global warming is and why, they know how hepatitis is spread, they follow labour and trade issues in the newspaper, they check quarterly reports to see how their mutual funds are fairing. Or not.

But they know about nutrition too, and they're so busy they don't always bother.

So this chapter is another run at Support as a Viable Role for Parents. Stock the fridge. Get lots of those little plastic juice containers that are recyclable and are always getting lost. Don't complain too much about the thermoses that break. And make sure they always have an emergency quarter or a phone card to call you if they need to.

In the general tips department, there's the thing about freezing your juicebox or juice container, to pack in the lunch the next day. This is truly great in summer and truly less great in winter when you will also have to pack a spoon to eat the slushy that you have instead of juice. A good, insulated lunchbag is worth the extra cost but gets lost just as well as the cheap version. The plastic lunch boxes that have the plastic thermos inside are not worth the money: the thermoses don't hold heat or cold and usually leak anyway.

The salad recipes below make enough for several lunches. Whip something up on Sunday and eat it Monday and Wednesday. Offer supper leftovers in the handy thermos. Keep a variety of buns, croissants, bagels and breads in the freezer, pre-cut. Recycle leftover pasta as salad, with a few fresh vegetables and a dressing.

Monday

*cranberry juice

*sliced turkey on a bun with lettuce, mayo, apple slices. Leftover stuffing from the Sunday roast is nice if you have it.

*small recyclable tub of yogourt with any fresh fruit cut into it. I mean, buy the large container of yogourt and put a cup or so of it into the container, and add fruit. Or you can buy those personal size yogourt containers, with fruit on the bottom, or the ones with granola on the top.

*cookies or brownie or cake or whatever you have, whether store bought or homemade.

Or:
*pear juice
*almond butter and apple butter on a raisin bagel
* yogourt cup (see above)

*Carrot salad
      4 or 5 sweet carrots, grated coarsely
      the juice of ½ lemon
      ¼ cup of vegetable oil (canola, olive, sunflower seed...)
      salt and pepper to taste
      1 teaspoon of black mustard seeds (black are prettier, but the
      yellow ones are fine too)

Mix this all together in a bowl. Keeps for days, at least enough for two lunches.

*Oatmeal cookies

This is a very balanced lunch: lots of protein in the almond butter, as well as the grain/dairy combination.

Tuesday

*apricot juice
*thermos of miso soup

*Wheat Berry, Lentil and Bean Salad
      1 cup of wheat berries (or brown rice)
      ½ cup of green lentils
      fistful of fresh green beans (a tin is ok)
      ¼ cup of parsley (or cilantro)
      1 tablespoon of sesame seeds (toasted is nice)
      1½ tablespoons of soya sauce
      ¼ cup of vegetable oil (sunflower seed)

Trim the green beans of their little stems and chop them into one-inch lengths. Put them into 2½ cups of boiling water for 3 minutes.

Save the cooking water. Remove the beans from the water, and lay them out loosely on your countertop to cool.

In a saucepan, stir the wheat berries or brown rice and lentils with a little oil. Add the bean cooking water and bring to a boil. Cover the pan, reduce heat to low, and cook until tender, about 40 minutes.

Combine berries or rice, drained beans (if using tinned beans, rinse them first), coarsely chopped parsley or cilantro, and dressing ingredients. Stir.

Keeps several days, doesn't get wilted in the lunchbox.

Alternatively:

*apple juice
*ham and Swiss on a bun with lettuce and dijon mustard
*bran muffin
*tomatoes, sliced, in a little tub, with salt or vinaigrette
*box of raisins

Wednesday

*drinking yogurt
*pita bread with hummos and alfalfa sprouts rolled up like a
    burrito (grated mozzarella in the mix is optional)
*Toss in an apple, or be expansive with:

*Fruit Salad

> 1 orange, peeled and cut in chunks
> 1 ruby grapefruit, peeled and cut in chunks
> 1 tin of artichoke hearts, quartered
> ½ cup of coriander leaves, chopped
> ½ red onion, very finely sliced in rings
> (Optional: handful beansprouts, cubed mango or avocado)

Dressing:

> 2 tablespoons of rice vinegar
> 1 inch cube ginger, peeled and grated
> 1 garlic clove, finely chopped
> ¼ cup of sunflowerseed oil
> a pinch of red chili flakes
> salt and pepper to taste

In a bowl, combine salad ingredients and in a cup, mix the
dressing. Combine and let marinate 15 minutes or up to 3 days.
Serves 4 and keeps well in the lunchbox.

Alternatively:

*fruit soda (or bottled fruit drink)
*tuna salad on whole wheat with spinach leaves, mayo, capers
    maybe
*bunch of grapes (in a container)

Sick of sandwiches? How about:

*Couscous salad
    1 cup of dry couscous
    1½ cups of chicken stock or water
    1 tin of chick peas, rinsed and drained
    1 handful of fresh parsley, chopped

Dressing:
    juice of 1 lemon
    ⅓ cup of canola oil or olive oil
    salt and pepper to taste
    small clove of garlic, minced

Bring the stock or water to the boil and pour it into a bowl over the couscous. Stir and let sit until the liquid is absorbed. Add chickpeas and parsley.

Assemble the dressing, mix well, and pour over the grain. Serves four and is lovely with a blob of harissa.

Thursday

*V-8 or other vegetable juice
*Tortellini, cheese stuffed, with pesto like a salad, in a little tub

*Different Fruit Salad:
    4 nectarines, pitted and sliced (or peaches)
    4 kiwi, peeled and sliced (grapes would do)
    10 sliced strawberries (or another berry, whole)

Dressing:
    ½ cupof yogourt
    2 tablespoons of frozen orange juice concentrate
    1 tablespoon of poppyseeds
    2 tablespoons of sugar

Mix the dressing together, pour over the mélange de fruits, and it's wonderful. Keeps beautifully for a day. Thereon, it slides downhill.

Or else:
* Edensoy drink box

*Tofu Salad with Hijiki:
    25 grams of dried hijiki seaweed (a cupful)
    1 square of firm tofu
    2 -3 cold baked beets, peeled and sliced
    1 handful of snow peas (or a cup of frozen peas)
    2 green onions, slivered

Dressing:
    2 tablespoons of soya sauce
    ¼ cup of sunflower seed or peanut oil
    1 tablespoon of grated ginger
    a few drops of sesame oil (optional)

Soak the seaweed in boiled water for 15 minutes, and drain. This water could be used for soup. Rinse and drain the tofu, and chop into little squares. Cut up the orange, stem the snow peas, and put these together in a bowl with the green onion.
Mix the dressing and pour it over the salad.

Variations:

    1 orange, peeled and chopped
    sunflower seeds, or sesame seeds, or cashews toasted
    (cilantro is a good addition)
    water chestnuts, peeled and sliced
    daikon or carrots, grated
    red pepper.

* Rice noodles with peanut sauce
Soak dry rice vermicelli in cold water for 2 hours or until soft. Drain. Dump on a few tablespoons of peanut sauce. *Voilà.*

Friday

*Fresh orange juice

*Granola
      3 cups of rolled oats
      1 cup of toasted sunflower seeds
      1 cup of roasted peanuts
      1 cup of wheat germ
      1 cup of unsweetened coconut
      ¼ cup of toasted sesame seeds
      ½ cup of honey
      ½ cup of oil
      sprinkle of salt
      1 cup of raisins

Spread the sunflower seeds and sesame seeds on a tray in your toaster oven for a time similar to "light toast", and then bring them out to cool. The toaster retains a lot of heat, and you have to bring your seed out of there or it will scorch, even after the dinger has dinged.

Heat the oil and honey together in a saucepan. When runny, pour over the other ingredients in a large bowl, EXCEPT the raisins, and then spread that all on a cookie sheet and pop it in the oven at 350°F for about 15 minutes. When things look toasty, stir, give it 10 more minutes and bring out of the oven, back into the bowl, and add the raisins. Let cool and store in jars.

Fantastically yummy with milk or yogourt, but good as a trail snack, on its own.

*tub de Yogourt (as on Monday), suitable for mixing with granola,
      if desired.
*carrot muffin

Sandwiches

So, I realize I'm only scratching the surface on the lunchboxes. Here are some other possibilities to choose from.

Artichoke Salad

Split your kaiser or focaccia or French stick or hot dog bun or whatever it is you have and pull out some of the bread from inside. Brush with olive oil or mayo to guard against sogginess, and spoon in a fairly lavish quantity of the following salad. Cut the sandwich in two, wrap, and place with pride in your child's lunchbox.

  1 tin of artichoke hearts, drained
  2 tablespoons of pickled capers, drained
  ½ red bell pepper
  1 nice tomato, drained, no seeds
  ½ cup of parsley
  ½ clove of garlic, minced
  ½ teaspoon of oregano or basil, if you like it better
  1 cup of grated mozzarella cheese
  salt and pepper at will
  1 tablespoon of red vinegar (balsalmic is nice, but so is wine vini)
  2 tablespoons of olive oil

Draining is important. Then chop everything fairly small. Chop up the bread that you removed from the sandwich bun and mix it with everything else on the list together in a bowl. Eventually construct your nice sandwiches, as described above.

This salad keeps pretty well refrigerated in an airtight plastic thing, for maybe four days.

You wouldn't make the sandwiches wait four days, though, would you? Yike, soggy.

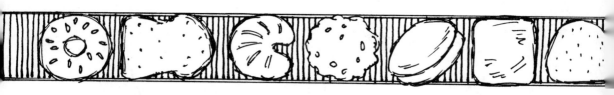

A Great Many Other Sandwich Possibilities

in a little Italian bun, that is brushed with olive oil.

1) avocado and grilled pepper, with pesto and ripe sliced avocado, on the bread, with the peeled sliced red pepper on top, and luxurious dabs of pesto on top of that, followed by the bun top.

❖ ❖ ❖

2) boiled egg, sliced, with lettuce and mayo, which is really somewhat self-explanatory. "Relatively straight-forward," we used to say in science class.

❖ ❖ ❖

3) grilled, sliced eggplant and provolone. Now, these are really made for each other. Slice the eggplant, salt it, let it sit in a colander for a half hour to sweat. Dry it off, brush with olive oil, broil on one side until brown, turn and broil the other side, take it out and let it cool. This is dense in flavour, sweet, and delicious, hot or cold. The provolone just accents it perfectly.

❖ ❖ ❖

4) mushroom and mozzarella, with a little soya. Now ideally, this is a hot melted sandwich, but it's not too shabby served cool. A few sesame and sunflower seeds on top during the melting part are very nice, hot or cold. If you like hot pickled peppers, this is where to put them.

❖ ❖ ❖

5) sprout, tomato, avocado and havarti, with a sprinkling of sesame, and some dots of tamari. Who here remembers the Cosmic Sandwich?… It's very quiet, humm. A great sandwich, however, in the late sixties at Rochdale College on Bloor Street in Toronto. And on a slice of multi-grain bread, HELLISHLY good for us.

❖ ❖ ❖

6) tomato, mozzarella, fresh basil is a summer bonanza. That heavenly scent of tomatoes warmed in the sunshine? Help! Olive oil or mayo on the bun protects from sogginess, lubricates and accents.

❖ ❖ ❖

7) zucchini with walnut purée is very nice. Slice the zuccs lengthwise thinly and fry in olive oil, although raw is okay too. Salt and pepper and mayo. This "walnut purée" is just walnuts in a food processor, with salt, some chopped parsley, and enough water to make it spin around. Chilies to taste.

Gorgeous Layered Focaccia Sandwiches

Another way to have thousands of variations.

You can buy a fresh focaccia loaf at your bakery, or use the pizza dough recipe mentioned somewhere here.

To prepare it, don't roll out the dough as for pizza (page 127), but just press it out into a shape about 12 inches in diameter. Dimple the top with your finger in a dozen places over the surface. Brush with olive oil, sprinkle with coarse salt, and rosemary or oregano, and let it rise on a cornmeal-sprinkled cookie sheet or in a 10-inch springform pan for a half hour or so.

Bake as for pizza, and let cool for a half hour.

Cut in half horizontally, to make two large thin circles of bread. Put whatever fillings you want inside, replace the top, and, optionally, warm in the oven briefly to melt whatever cheese you have used.

Cut into wedges and serve.

Possible Fillings:

1) roasted red pepper, feta cheese, arugula leaves
2) pesto, baked tomato purée, grated mozzarella
3) slices of grilled eggplant, hummos and provolone cheese
4) fried fennel slices, baked garlic puree, chèvre
5) tampenade (olive spread), sliced tomatoes, edam slices
6) smoked turkey slices, mayo, lettuce, cranberry sauce

You can imagine, there are some others.

CHAPTER NINE

Party Snacks You Can Make While Talking on the Phone

Your teens are hosting and going to parties, to raves, to dinners with their boy/girlfriends. They have to eat something besides a bag of chips. They also have to get the makeup on and the hair right and directions for the bike/car/subway ride. So here are some no-brainer recipes for excellent food they can serve at home or take away.

Sesame Beans

1 pound of fresh green beans
¼ cup of sunflower seed oil
1 teaspoon of sesame oil
2 tablespoons of Kikkoman or another light soya sauce
2 tablespoons of sesame seeds

Snap the stems off the beans but leave the little tips on the other end. They're pretty, and they have most of the vegetable's nutrition. Drop the beans in a pot of boiling salted water for two minutes, drain and refresh the beans under cold water. Drain again.

Place the sesame seeds on a tray or on aluminum foil in your toaster oven. Toast as you would for light toast and then let cool.

Combine the oils and soya sauce in a bowl and add the beans. Stir to coat the beans and let this marinate for a while. Then place the beans attractively on your serving platter and sprinkle them with the sesame seeds. Voilà.

◆　◆　◆

Asparagus Wrapped in Prosciutto

1 pound of fresh asparagus
¼ pound of thinly sliced proscuitto ham
juice of one lime

Snap the tough tips off the thick (not the flowery-looking) end of each asparagus spear. You do this by holding the tough tip in Hand 'A', and while holding the middle of the spear in Hand 'B', rotating Wrist 'A' clockwise. Cagey move, no? Perhaps drawings would be good. Arrows and insets.

Fling rinsed spears into boiling salted water for 2 minutes, drain, stop their cooking by plunging in cold water, and drain again. On a platter, squeeze the juice of one lime over top of the cooling fellows and let marinate.

Choose a thin slice of prosciutto and roll it around one or more asparagus spears. Place festively back on the platter and roll up the others in the same way. Now you're done.

Mushrooms on Toast with Havarti Cheese, Sesame and Kikkoman

Somewhat self-explanatory perhaps, but very good.

1 pound of fresh mushrooms, plain white ones, or brown, sliced
ten slices of caraway rye bread toasted
½ pound of Danish havarti cheese sliced
2 tablespoons of sesame seeds toasted
Kikkoman or another light soya sauce
red chili flakes and ground black pepper

Halve each slice of toast and arrange them on a cookie sheet. Put a little pile of sliced mushrooms on top of each, slices of cheese on top of the mushrooms, and sprinkle sesame seeds over that. Place in the 350°F oven until the cheese melts, maybe 4 or 5 minutes. Put the canapés on a platter and sprinkle with Kikkoman, chilies, and pepper if you like them.

Portobellos with Gorgonzola

A match made in heaven.

small portobello mushrooms (see just below for quantity)
a little wedge of gorgonzola cheese (I'll get to this in a minute)
olive oil for frying
2 cloves of garlic, chopped, should be enough

How many people are you feeding? Use one or two small portobellos for each one, or if you only find the huge ones, figure a half for each person, maybe. Use the French gorgonzola. It's very good for melting, and it's half the cost of the Italian stuff. It's still pretty darned expensive, but this creamy blue cheese is incredibly delicious.

So. You brush the mushrooms free of compost and you snap off the stems. Save the stems for something; they're too good to throw away. Heat the olive oil in a big frypan over medium heat and pop in your whole or halved mushroom caps. Cook until browning on one side and flip over. Now add the chopped garlic and stir things around until the mushrooms are getting soft. Put little chunks of gorgonzola on each upturned cap and cover the pan for 2 or 3 minutes until the cheese is melting. Sprinkle with salt and pepper and serve.

Salsas

What is salsa, reall, a condiment, or a diced salad? Huh.

Tomatillo Salsa

2 cups of tomatillos with the papery skins removed
1 tomato, seeded and chopped
juice of one lime
½ teaspoon of red chili flakes (or 2 fresh seeded chopped jalapenos)
½ cup of fresh coriander leaves, chopped
1 clove of garlic, minced
2 green onions, chopped finely

Rinse the peeled tomatillos and chop them up coarsely. Add the other ingredients and let rest for at least an hour before serving. The day before is okay.

Thai Salsa

1 beautiful green mango, peeled and diced
2 inches of ginger, peeled and grated
2 cloves of garlic, minced
½ teaspoon red chili flakes, my favourite
1 whole green onion, chopped finely
juice and grated peel of 1 lime
½ cup each of fresh mint, coriander and basil leaves, chopped
splash of fish sauce

Combine all these incredibly lovely ingredients and serve after about an hour of marinating time, as a condiment to chicken or fish, or as a tiny salad beside Vietnamese Spring Rolls (see page 115) .

Fresh Salsa

1 large tomato, seeded and chopped finely
2 jalapeno peppers, seeded and chopped finely, or 1 teaspoon dried
    chili flakes
1 green bell pepper, seeded and chopped finely
½ white onion, peeled and chopped finely
2 cloves of garlic, minced
juice of 1 lime or 4 teaspoons of vinegar
½ cup of chopped cilantro
½ cup of tomato sauce
salt and black pepper to taste

Stir ingredients in a steel or glass bowl and let sit for an hour.
Great with chips or quesadilla or chili or guacamole or black bean
soup or wherever. I draw the line at cereal, however; it's lost on rice
krispies.

More Mangos

Mango Salsa II

2 ripe mangos, peeled, pitted and cubed
½ English cucumber, chopped small
2 jalapeno chilies, seeded and diced
½ cup of coriander leaves, rinsed and chopped

Combine all ingredients and let marinate for at least a half hour.
Check for salt before serving with any fried food.

Mango Salsa III

2 ripe mangos, peeled, pitted and chopped
3 sweet peppers, a red, yellow and green, seeded and chopped
½ red onion, chopped
¼ cup of coriander leaves, chopped
½ cup of peanuts (toasted is nice)
juice of a lime
½ teaspoon of red chili flakes

Combine ingredients and let sit for a half hour. Incredible with fish or chicken, as a condiment in any Southeast Asian supper, and with spring rolls.

Tzatziki

Tzatziki made from goats' milk tastes sublime and fills the bill for some people who have allergies to cows' milk products.

1 500 millilitre container of yogourt (goat or cow)
1 clove of garlic (minced finely—this is a tip)
¼ cup of diced cucumber
1 teaspoon each of ground cumin and salt

Line a sieve or colander with a clean dish cloth and set over a bowl. Empty the contents of the yogourt container into this sleeve and let it drip, in a cool place, for at least 2 or 3 hours. Longer is fine: I would refrigerate it and just cover the top of the yogourt with a damp cloth if I were leaving it overnight.

Discard the liquid that has separated into the bowl. The remaining yogourt is quite thick, and you have to scrape it off the sieve-liner cloth, into a bowl, to which you add the other ingredients. Stir it up and then let it rest in the fridge for another hour or so to let the flavours come up.

Raita

So delicious and standard at any Punjabi feast.

1 500 millilitre container of yogourt
1 English cucumber, diced, or field cuke if you peel and seed it
2 tablespoons of fresh mint, minced
1 teaspoon of salt
1 teaspoon of ground cumin
¼ teaspoon of both cayenne and black pepper

Drain your yogourt, as above for the tzatziki, and drain the cucumber too. Add the other stuff.

Other Things to do with Drained Yogourt

Having hung your yogourt, you can add lots of other things to spread on crackers or serve with fruit. Salt the cheese lightly, too.

*dill, chopped and mixed with the yogourt, served with figs or melon
*crushed black pepper, serve with Scandinavian crisps
*green onions and coriander, also great with crisp bread

There are variations from many of the Middle Eastern countries. It's a great condiment, and a traditional way to get milk protein in a hot place.

❖ ◆ ◆

Hummos

Repeated, since every party can use some.

½ cup of dry chick peas or a tin, ready to go
1½ cups of water
a bay leaf
juice of a lemon
2 teaspooons of ground cumin
1 teaspoon of minced garlic
3 tablespoons of tahini (ground sesame seeds, check your local
    grocery store)
2 tablespoons of sunflower seed oil or another oil
salt to taste

Put the chick peas and the bay leaf in a saucepan with the water, cover the pan and bring the water to a boil. Turn off the heat, and let rest for a half hour. This brings the peas to the same point they'd be if you'd soaked them overnight.

Check that the peas are still covered with water. Turn on the heat again and simmer them gently, covered, for 45 minutes or until they're really tender.

Or, skip this part by opening a tin of chickpeas and rinsing them very well.

Remove the bay leaf and purée the chickpeas in a food processor with as much cooking liquid or additional water as is needed to make a thick paste. Add the lemon juice, cumin, tahini, oil and salt, and serve it with whole wheat pita bread pieces or toast.

Artichoke Dip

A down-home recipe for the buffet.

1 tin of artichoke hearts, drained and chopped
1 cup of light mayonnaise
½ cup of grated parmesan cheese
½ cup of grated cheddar
½ teaspoon of paprika
½ cup of walnut pieces

Stir together chokes, mayo, cheese and paprika and dump into microwavable container. Sprinkle walnuts on top, cover with vented plastic wrap and nuke 6 minutes on HIGH. Gorgeous. Dip fresh Italian bread into it.

Caponata

1 tin of chick peas, drained and rinsed
1 roasted red sweet pepper, peeled and seeded
1 clove of garlic, coarsely chopped
juice of a half lemon
¼ cup of olive oil
2 tablespoons of tahini

Put the whole thing in the food processor and let 'er rip until smooth. Delicious and good for us.

Guacamole

Mash up a ripe (tender, not soft) peeled, pitted avocado with a fork. Add nothing. Well, maybe the juice of half a lime, and it's perfect.

But, if you must, add a tablespoon each of chopped green onion and finely chopped fresh coriander. Salt and pepper to taste. Garlic, all right, one small finely chopped clove. Some people have to have a half tomato, diced, and a seeded, minced, jalapeno pepper. It's gilding the lily, but okay. Guacamole is a personal thing, and you make what you want.

Raw Things

Gravlax

This is home-cured fish. Salmon is the most common, but you could experiment with trout or another fatty fish.

2 half pound salmon filets or so, boned, each about the same size
½ cup each of white sugar and coarse salt
1 tablespoon each of peppercorns and coriander seed
1 bunch of fresh coriander leaf (dill is nice too)
1 cup or so of olive oil

Rinse the fish and dry. Coarsely grind the pepper and coriander seed, like, really just break open the seeds, that's enough. Mix the salt, sugar and spices together. Rinse and dry the green leaves, and remove any big stems.

Lay a plastic bag in a pieplate, with the opening up. Place ⅓ of the greenery in the bottom of the bag. Sprinkle half the salt/sugar/spice mixture (hereafter to be called "the salt") on top. Lay one of your salmon filets on top of that, skin side down. Sprinkle the flesh side with some of "the salt", and put another third of the green leaves on top of that. Aside, sprinkle the other filet flesh with "the salt", and lay it, flesh side down, in the bag. Put the rest of "the salt" on the skin side and lay the last of the greens on top of that. Close the bag.

Now, you need a brick. A big tin will do. Place that on top of the fish in the bag and refrigerate the whole mess for three days. You have to turn the bag over every 12 hours.

In three days, the salt will draw the moisture out of the fish, and it will have a dense, stiff texture. Drain the fish, break off the marinade, and slice the fish as thinly as you can, on the diagonal, placing each slice in a nice glass serving bowl (we use a butter dish with a lid). Cover the fish with olive oil.

This will keep 10 days, refrigerated. Use it as you would smoked salmon, even just set the whole dish out on a platter, flanked by crackers or bread or Belgium endive leaves. It's nice too as a canapé with a sweet mustardy vinaigrette.

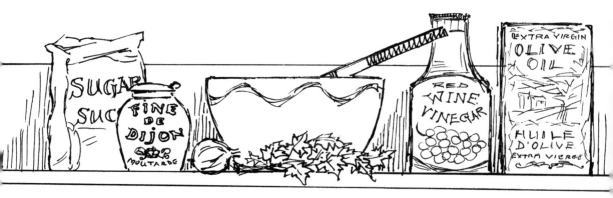

Mustard Sauce

1 tablespoon of dijon mustard
2 tablespoons of red wine vinegar
2 teaspoons of minced shallot
¼ cup of fresh coriander leaf finely chopped, or another leaf like
     dill, parsley, or tarragon
¾ cup of olive oil
1 tablespoon of white sugar
salt and pepper to taste

In a mixing bowl, whisk together the shallot, mustard and vinegar.
In a very thin stream, add the olive oil, WHILE WHISKING. Take
your time. You'll end up with something like a yellow mayonnaise.
Add the sugar, s&p, and herb. Stir to blend and serve beside your
gravlax with a spoon.

Carpaccio

Lots of ways to serve this, but the following is the basic idea. This makes enough for 15.

1 pound eye of round (beef)
½ pound of parmesan reggiano in a piece, (the real stuff is really
    so much better)
¼ cup of good olive oil—blow the wad, get extra virgin
black pepper, freshly ground
capers, black olives, chopped anchovies, arugula leaves all optional
crusty Italian bread not very optional

When you get home from the grocery store, freeze your eye of round. That's it for today.

❖   ❖   ❖

Okay, if you're in a rush, just freeze it for an hour. Get a really sharp knife, and without once removing any of your fingers, slice the meat as thinly as you can. With the meat half frozen like this, you can slice it pretty darned thin. Place the slices attactively on a serving platter, and keep it cool.

Ready to serve? Adorn the platter with a few arugula (or another lettuce) leaves, tucking them under the meat, or skip that part—it doesn't matter. Grind a lot of black pepper on there, and drizzle on the olive oil. Grate the parmesan, in nice long flakes, with a potato peeler. (You could also use the side of your grater that has just those two blades?) Arrange the flakes on the meat.

To finish, sprinkle on either (not all) a few capers, or black olives, or chopped anchovies. If you have none of these, you could sprinkle on a LITTLE coarse salt, if you must. It's pretty darned perfect as it is. Put the carpaccio on the table with (warm) crusty bread nearby. People will figure it out.

Salads on the Buffet

Or "What's Tupperware For, Anyway?"

Black Beans with Refreshing Other Things

1 cup of dry black beans (or a tin, rinsed)
½ an English cucumber, chopped
1 ripe avocado, peeled, seeded, chopped
half a red onion, sliced very thinly
juice of two limes
⅔ cup of sunflower seed oil
1 or 2 cloves of garlic, minced
¼ cup of fresh coriander leaf, chopped
salt and pepper to taste
a teaspoon of sugar is optional

If you are opting for the dry black beans, God bless you. Boil them gently in three cups of water with a bay leaf until they are tender, about an hour. Drain.

If you are using the tinned beans, okay for you. Wash them nicely, and they will be just fine.

In a bowl, combine all the ingredients and stir. This salad is wonderful for one day only. If you want to make it in advance, add the cucumber and avocado in the last hour or two before serving.

Wild Rice Salad with Oranges

½ cup of dry wild rice
2 tablespoons of wheat berries
2 cups of water or stock
2 oranges, peeled and sliced
½ cup of pecans toasted
2 green onions chopped
¼ cup of fresh mint chopped

Dressing:
½ cup of sunflower seed oil
3 tablespoons of Kikkoman or another light soya sauce
1 teaspoon of fresh ginger, grated

Rinse the rice and berries (whole wheat kernels) in a sieve under running water and then add to a saucepan of stock and boil gently for 40 minutes, until the rice grains split. Drain and let the rice cool.

In a jar, shake together the dressing ingredients. In a bowl, combine the orange pieces, onions, mint, nuts, and rice, and pour the dressing over. Toss and serve.

Dandelion Salad

This is so easy. We used to putter in the yard getting the first spring dandelion leaves, they're very yummy, but now you can go to the store for cultivated dandilion, which is also good, and available year-round.

1 bunch of fresh dandelion leaves
4 hard-boiled eggs sliced, call them "detectives"
½ red onion, thinly sliced

Dressing:
2 tablespoons of red wine vinegar
2 teaspoons of mustard
¼ cup of olive oil or another oil
salt and pepper as you like it

Wash and drain leaves, chop them into bite-sized lengths and fling them in your salad bowl of choice. Whisk up the dressing, pour it on, add the onion and mix this all together. Top with the detectives. Also nice with crisp bacon atop.

Greek Salad

I live in a Greek neighbourhood, which means there are 500,000 places to hang out at night on a warm sidewalk, with food. This salad is a mainstay.

1 head of romaine lettuce or iceberg, if you like
½ white onion, sliced thinly
½ English cucumber, chopped, or a field cuke, peeled and seeded
1 green pepper, seeded and chopped thinly
2 green onions, trimmed and chopped
2 ripe tomatoes, cut in eighths
½ pound of feta cheese, crumbled
1 cup of black olives, the small calamata are fine

Dressing:
¼ cup of red wine vinegar
1 teaspoon of dried oregano leaf
salt and pepper to taste
¾ cup of olive oil

Combine the last four ingredients in a jar, shake it up vigorously, and taste. It should be quite tart without making your eyes water. Add a little more oil if you hate it.

Wash and drain the lettuce. Slice each leaf down the centre rib and then chop all of them crosswise in 1" wide strips. I don't care what they say about using a knife on lettuce. Add all the other stuff on top, except the cheese. Pour on the dressing when you are ready to serve, not sooner, and toss. The salad will wilt slowly once the dressing is on. Garnish with the cheese and serve with pride.

Greek Salad for 100

You can do this.

20 to 25 heads of romaine or iceberg
10 cucumbers
20 bunches of green onions
20 tomatoes
20 green peppers
2 heads of celery
1 little barrel of kalamata olives
2 kilos of feta cheese, crumbled

All this you wash and trim. Divide evenly and store lettuce in four clean plastic grocery bags. Other ingredients mingled in another bag, ready to dump on top.

Dressing
1 3-litre container of oil (olive is best, though it's dear)
2 litres of red wine vinegar (try to get Greek vini—it's so good)
1½ cups of salt
1 cup of black pepper
1 cup of dried oregano
¼ cup of chopped garlic

Assemble and shake vigorously in air-tight plastic containers.
  When ready to assemble, dump out the lettuce into a huge bowl, shake on a portion of the vegetables, dress with the vinaigrette, and toss to mix. Then throw overtop about a pound of crumbled feta and two handfuls of olives. This has worked for us at our school Fun Fair, and t sells like crazy.

If it's easier, make the dressing in four batches.
Per batch, combine:

3 cups of oil
2 cups of vinegar
⅓ cup of salt
¼ cup of pepper
¼ cup of oregano
3 tablespoons of garlic

There's pleasure in variety. Your kids find out about the world of food and they'll explore it, fool around with it, and sustain themselves with it in the physical sense, as well as the metaphorical one.

My mother was embarrassed once in her teens: she was asked if she would like her tea with lemon or with milk. She wasn't sure and said "Both." Her tea curdled, and she swore her children would avoid a similar moment, would know the rules. Kindly, she made sure we all do.

I figure, along the same lines, that kids should know about the world of flavour. There's a whole lot more out there than what comes in a box, and it's fun to access it. It's a small road to the globe, but the globe is getting very small.

◆   ◆   ◆

The upshot here is the wonder of parenthood, the morphological miracle and the getting to know your relatives. They keep you going, don't they? They don't play by the rules, don't like your lemon custard, want the oversized jeans, give you little love poems for your birthday and make you laugh till you fall over.

I like to cook, and now, so do the kids. We'll always have something we can do together.

Index of Recipes

NOTES

NOTES

NOTES